I0474519

Freeflow Books
Copyright ©2015
ISBN: 978-1508871521
Library of Congress Catalog Card Number: No!
All rights reserved.

Cover design by Rose Throop

I dedicate this volume to the many people who are much braver than I. Those who look down into the eyes of corrupt power, and spit.

Must Stop the Lower Order of Humanity

I need to get lots of these nature paintings finished before the final assault on the flora and fauna of Central New York. If you live in New York, Syracuse, Rochester, Albany, Buffalo, Binghamton or Utica cities, if you squat on a small backyard, or public park and have factory beef and chicken barbecues and raise babies where the urban veil often blinds you to the natural truth of things, yet still feel that pesky on-and-off pulse of sentiment for life outside of your bubble metropolita, please consider offering a fleeting several seconds of your busy day to the collective mind torture of the men who want to sell you natural gas.

Let's mark a time. Say 3:24 p.m.?

Maybe strong dream justice is all we ever needed to achieve miracles.

Here we are at an infinitesimal point in earth's infinity cycle when mind justice may be our only hope beyond the terror of some real bad collective practices warping out of control.

I am so tired of feeling powerless. Let's sleep on this together. And dream!

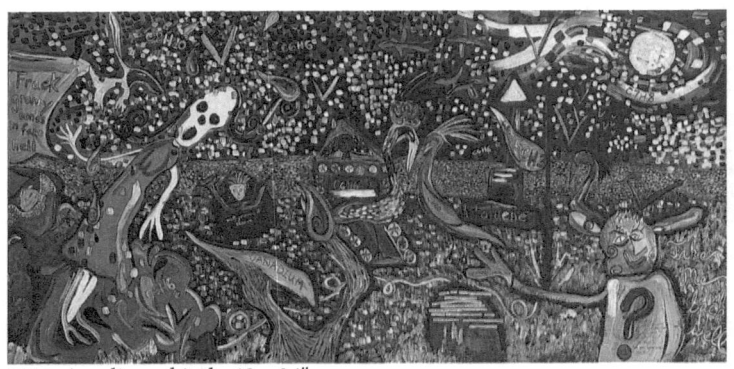

2011. Acrylic on birch, 48 x 24"

Frack Immaculata!

I am taking art to the level it was meant to be. Presently I am documenting our last battle.

I am one man, one artist insane, crazy enough to place the entire hydro-fracking debate onto my shoulders. I have taken up a position, and now will give the only argument morally acceptable. I shall schlop onto canvas, paper, and hardboard the property rapists of my country in all the colors of their inside organs and respective juices. After viewing my show, all pro-fracking dreams will blow out of the state quicker than the greedy butt-crack stampede from Texas that brought them here.

I shall not take up a scientific argument on the process. Hydraulic fracturing of the Marcellus Shale has the potential of poisoning the groundwater for hundreds of thousands of people for many generations. A man need only hear this news once to react. Just using the logic of foraging black bears would measure some intelligent questions to follow. Who is to profit from these drilling ventures? Is it true that there are cases where tap water out west can be ignited from a faucet? What are the chemicals used in the process? Why doesn't the industry have to disclose them publicly? Pushing millions of gallons of freshwater laced with up to a hundred chemicals (known and unknown) into the rock bed under high pressure to release mass quantities of methane just doesn't sound that safe, does it? I mean, even to a moron, or an alcoholic, or wife beater. So why does the Governor of New York State allow this kind of Texas oilman trespass upon his constituents? True, the silent-majority of Americans are mostly short-sighted and selfish, always ready with an opinion on either side of the death debate.

Farmer Ted: "A hundred grand a lease? That's powerful money. I don't want government telling me who not to poison. Where do I sign?"

Governor Andrew: "Eight million to my super PAC? Screw New York infants!"

I am working on a painting to shame the governor out of his fine Italian suit. I have the bones of his grandmother, Immaculata, in a red dress, being shot from her Long Island grave by a geyser of liquid carcinogens. Some shore birds and other funny creatures are hanging out in the cemetery on a moonlit night. Words across the sky might read: "Hey Governor, We Sure Hope That Immaculata Isn't Fracked Out of the Very Ground You Saturate With Poison". We'll see what kind of reaction I get from our state boss. I will put on a price tag of six thousand dollars. Maybe he will buy it to destroy it. Half of the proceeds will pay my tax to the Onondaga. The other half will go toward a bigger painting of shame until the Governor uses his overpaid trooper gang to escort Texas oil the hell off our land.

Laissez-faire capitalism was a grand party for the chosen few during the 19th century. And it ran like a top beside the presence of cholera and death-by-childbirth. Such frequent miseries kept all survival joys in check. A slave workforce made anyone not a slave much too busy to oversee the rich neighbor's trespass. And the water was always dirty poop, for science had not yet escaped the confines of the Pentateuch. God took little Johnny because it was predestined to be. What matter that Grandma picked pole beans with fecal fingers? Or that they laid Johnny to rest with his lead toy soldier ten feet from the well-sweep? Suzy was next, and the family watched her every move with working dread.

Today we know better. We know a lot about the environment and the fragile balance that exists wherever man settles his toxic prejudice. Modern families don't pour known carcinogens into their wells for a paycheck. Yet for some wicked reason the government by the people, and for the people, wants to persuade the people to consider this action as an economic opportunity. Poison our kids and we will reap wonderful financial benefits. Instant winnings for the well leasers. Trickle-down, cheap energy for everyone else. A few, maybe even thirty dead kids, but all iPhones still humming at Cafe des Artistes on the Upper West Side.

Politics have officially warped into a vile adjunct of corporate power. The Governor knows hydrofracking has the potential to make all life around it sick and dying. He knows that the majority of his lunch friends are corrupt, negligent, and possibly homicidal in their dealings with the red-faced Texans and their high greed agenda. Yet he still touts childhood cancer as a regretful, albeit necessary result of hydraulic fracturing.

We who matter should have our legs sawed off for being such cowards. Why is my call for immediate arrest of the Governor ignored? He should be unkindly imprisoned for life for perpetuating this phony debate endangering the better health of our friends and families.

Another angle to consider is this: New York State government has no authority to offer these carpetbagging cheese faces high bid rights to our land. The chemical water shoots over boundaries, and seeps across roads.

It's a vote of no-confidence folks. Take a walk in the woods to reflect upon who has power over your family and friends. I shall start paying my tax to the true nation-state where throughout this life I rest my travel bones. The Onondaga base their policy decisions on how the seventh generation will be affected. Oh that is wise. And strong. The Governor could use a real father-chief to slap him down in shame before the rest of the tribe.

The dumb among us will take all of their neighbors to the justice of the Onondaga quicker than a frack-gush up the proverbial coke nose of avarice

We are so poisoned in the brain by this government we prop up by virtue of a coddled economy.

Here's a take from a long dead Atlantic traveler on how man has become a somewhat useful pawn of the present state:

After having thus successively taken each member of the community in its powerful grasp and fashioned him at will, the supreme power then extends its arm over the whole community. It covers the surface of society with a network of small complicated rules, minute and uniform, through which the most original minds and the most energetic characters cannot penetrate, to rise above the crowd. The will of man is not shattered, but softened, bent, and guided; men are seldom forced by it to act, but they are constantly restrained from acting. Such a power does not destroy, but it prevents existence; it does not tyrannize, but it compresses, enervates, extinguishes, and stupefies a people, till each nation is reduced to nothing better than a flock of timid and industrious animals, of which the government is the shepherd.
—de Tocqueville

Those local clans still bearing a conscience need to organize a mob. The land men want your land. The companies they represent want to see your babies get sick for a profit. A super biggie profit.

A hot dangy-dong-diddle-dee-doo kind of big fat Texas goo profit. A glass of cool, fresh indian water and not-so-indian carcinogenic compounds to quench a summer thirst. A Saturday night bath and a red rash tattoo for little coughing Tom and coffin Sue. What's it worth to you, shale squatters of the present moment? A temporary new smell in a shiny red pick-up? A pole barn envy? The NFL Sunday ticket?

They desire a hot ejaculation of benzene and phenol into your village groundwater. The Governor hovers above in a trooper chopper, rubbing his hands together in a show of fiendish glee. He longs to see all of you rurals heaped onto a pile. Your pathetic firehouse vote is laughable to the millions of Manahattas sucking the earth out from under your feet. A hundred grand to sicken my family for life? Really? That much, eh?

Okay, I'm in. Wait till they see my loaded Deere at the Grange. That hog Harold Hoenow will be green from envy, or that Vanadium cocktail he shared on the porch with Ruth.

No, I have to hope there is still a slurry of indigenous righteousness left swirling in our guts. Please good people temporarily living atop the ancient beds of shale, be kind and hospitable to the landmen at your door. A smile and a kind word is all anybody needs. And on a hot summer's day, a cold glass of lemon-lime aid sweetened with antifreeze wouldn't hurt either. It might teach these raunchy carpetbaggers to prey on their own kind back in the dumbed-down, drought-dried southlands.

They're coming to a door near you. Get 'em.

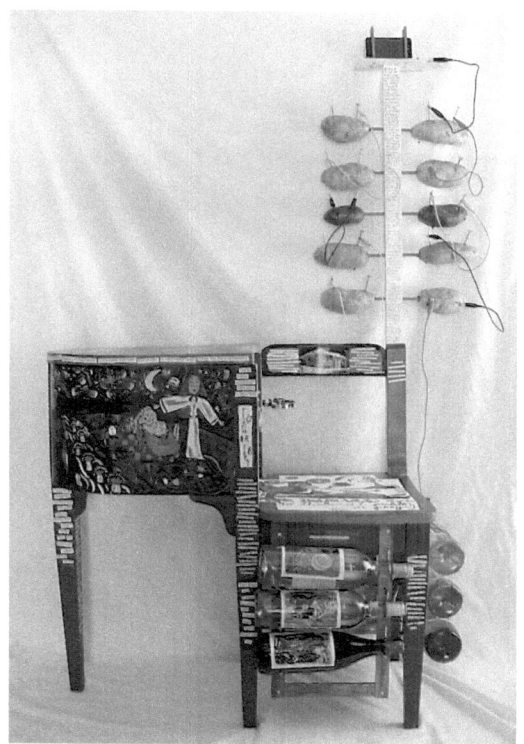

Armageddon Wine Bar 2010.
Acrylic on old telephone table

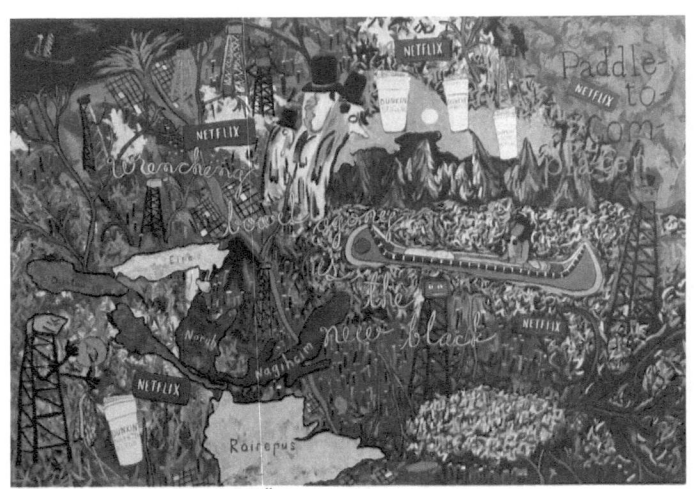

Acrylic on canvas, 57 x 40"

Paddle-To-Com-Pla-Cen-Cy

Divide and conquer. Offer a new John Deere to my namby-Bambi warrior neighbor and why should he care if a speculum was affixed to the mouths of every child outside his six acres, and benzene poured down their gullible gullets? He got his new tractor. That's good enough for him. German Hans got to keep his assembly line job at the plant too back in '44 as long as he didn't complain about the chain gang of Polish slaves out in the steel yard. Outside his sleepy village a smokestack exhaled overtime a peculiar smell that only rumor could define, but thought better left unsaid. Anyway Christmas was coming, and that kind of horror exposed would dampen the children's spirits.

New York State is poised to allow massive injections of benzene into the subterranean world which encases our ground water. Sometimes art and politics must mix else we do nothing but order coffee, watch Netflix, and wait for the dirty urban trend-setters to inform us ignorant country mice on taste, ad nauseum.

The gas lobbyist knows this game well. Copied right out of the playbook of the coal and oil magnates. Bring the local idiot a six-pack. After the second beer start praising his ignorance. Say something like deer hunting is a man thing to do and only sissies would think about the purity of their drinking water. Get him to laugh about prejudice or bigotry, pretend rage at the "liberals" in Washington who want to regulate progress, tell him how much you admire his countryman thinking and of course global warming can't be true if it ever snows. Get out the contract. Tell him the money prize. Look how stern and concentrated his thoughts while signing his name with your leader's golden pen.

Thank him toughly. Get into your rented F350. Drive over to the hotel holding your stack of signed contracts. Dress into your oxford shirt and BMW. Turn on satellite radio, and drive back home to wife and kids whom you love deeply.

Back home to any German town 1944.

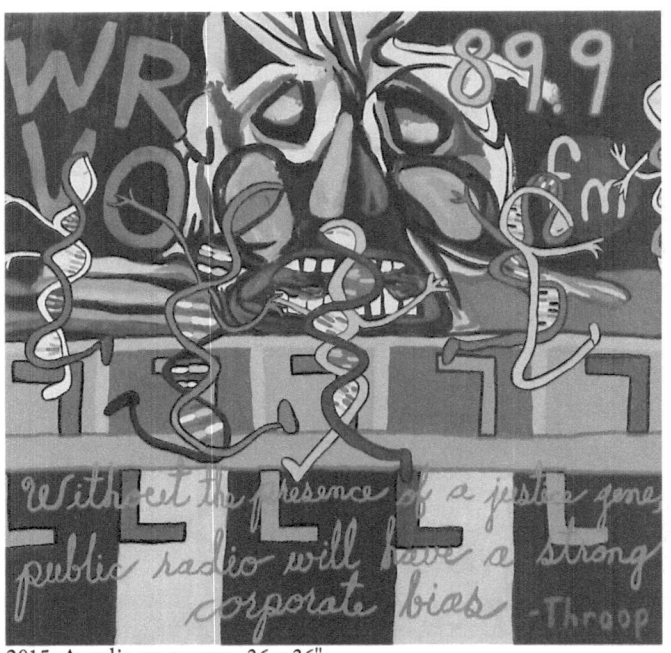

2015. Acrylic on canvas, 36 x 36"

Without The Presence of a Justice Gene, Public Radio Will Have a Strong Corporate Bias

Sonny Weston of Raphael's Restaurante, teenage chef and individual child hobo like myself, must have had an insight into the psyche of my future being when he would greet me every time with a fazed look and the spoken word, "why?". "Why Ron, why?" I guess it was my token expression among friends, my most used word during the discovery years of youth. Even my grandmother from her nursing home bed said I was an aspiring philosopher, and another friend, I forget who, called me Philosopher Ron. I remember getting punched in the cheek during a flash rumble and turning back to face my opponent to ask him, "Why, why did you just do that?"

My curiosity was most always human related. I certainly was not (am not) full of wonder, like a child asking, "What is the grass?" Unlike my practical teenage friends, I didn't care to know how a car engine worked, or how to attach a door to its jamb. However, I *was* concerned about human behavior. Why did my friend Kyle kick me in the balls just to show off to an older kid he wanted to impress? Why did Rich, the neglected suburban child-poet, decide that dairy farming beheld a bright future? Why did I end up being such an underachieving hoodlum when I wanted to be a forest ranger and had such a healthy lust for sports? Etcetera.

As I grew older, I pushed further with the whys. My first "A" in college was a class in sociology, above a "D" in calculus, and a "C" in accounting. Regrettably, I remained a business major for two more years until my first history elective. I changed majors, truly excited was I to find the answers that history provided. No gray area in hindsight. Kennedy slept with lots of women while he determined the fate of earth with nuclear testings. Hoover was an incompetent bully buffoon who swore that MLK was a communist because, according to Hoover's official federal psychosis, all black people who had cultural and political thoughts could only be communist.

Of course reading history just inflamed the "whys". I read literature, seeking more answers. Kurt Vonnegut was a "why" man.

Slaughterhouse 5 would lose all of its charm (and sales), but not much of its meaning, if Vonnegut published the word "why" on one page, and left it at that.

From literature, to psychology, and finally back to sociology. Stanley Milgram discovered more than an innate penchant for humanity to follow the leader. He unknowingly discovered the presence of a justice gene. That is my hypothesis anyway, and genetic research might not be too far off confirming it. For those not familiar with his work, Milgram ran tests at Yale in 1961 to determine how it was possible for thousands of ordinary Germans to carry out the holocaust. Read about his experiment. It alone has answered so many local and national "whys" for me. The potential of power and propaganda to shape public opinion is greater than the individual ability to think for oneself. All forty participants in his study put 300 volts (also labeled "Extreme Intensity Shock") into an actor because he was failing a word game, and the man wearing the lab coat in the electrocution room told them to proceed. From the other room the actor was crying out that he had enough, stop the experiment. 26 of the 40 took this torture up to 450 volts (past "Danger: Severe Shock"), several jolts after the actor went silent in the next room.

I believe that had Milgram tested a thousand people instead of forty, at least one would have stopped the moment an "ouch" was heard from the adjoining room. The other 999 would match similar results from the original 40 tested. That unfortunate person would possess what I call "the justice gene". I also surmise that testing teenagers would have skewed his results and shown more justice genes as a group; even more so among populations of Native Americans. I cannot imagine 26 out of 40 reservation Navajo juicing to death another Navajo because some goofy dude in a white coat told them to.

Anyway, to the painting.

I have that justice gene. It expressed itself as the ever present "why" when I was a boy. I know of it now while listening to National Propaganda Radio. The latter has contracted with America's Natural Gas Alliance to promote its agenda in exchange for the minds of the last hold out Americans. Their campaign is called "Think About It", and I believe its sole purpose is to normalize the potential disaster of hydrofracking among those who feel themselves sophisticated enough to listen to the man in the lab coat tell them how to think at any hour of the day. NPR and America's Natural Gas Alliance know that the game will be won, that it's just a matter of time. Every day I feel like the one in a thousand who wasn't asked to participate in the Milgram obedience experiment. By this, I also believe that any employee of NPR, and by association, my local public radio station, daily administers an "Extreme Intensity Shock" to his or her neighbor. None of them have ever asked why. They wait to be told what to say, and they broadcast it over the airwaves to 100,000 people.

So Sonny Weston, upon meeting up again 30 years late, please ask me "Why... why Ron, why?".

Because I fear in my heart of hearts dear Sonny, that without the presence of a justice gene, you my old friend, would fry me in a chair if the radio, television or the President told you to. I know that the propagandists know exactly what they are doing. Media programming has one universal agenda, whether it be broadcast by Rupert Murdoch's Fox TV, the *New York Times*, or geographically significant "little" WRVO, the public radio station. Their programming is meant to program you. Your thoughts are not your thoughts.

Or Sonny, today you may be a fan of pretend right wing talk radio. Say, Rush Limbaugh, who is NPR heavy as the latter is light on Limbaugh. He doesn't like anti-frackers either. He wants jobs too. There is no talk of Clean Energy Acts on his show, nor the effects of benzene in the water, or mile long 1-inch thick cement casing that need to hold its structure forever, even after the hundred mini-earthquakes have rattled its integrity. You will never hear of paid for in-your-face media stories on the dangers of hydrofracking. Both Rush and NPR forbid it. If you get any information, it will provide both side's issues of a manufactured debate. Yet turn on the radio to hear a well engineer talk of the dangers of hydrofracking, or a scientific explanation of half-life testings of fracking chemicals, and leave it at that? Never. All those smart guys have been obediently electrocuted. Silenced by the man in the white lab coat.

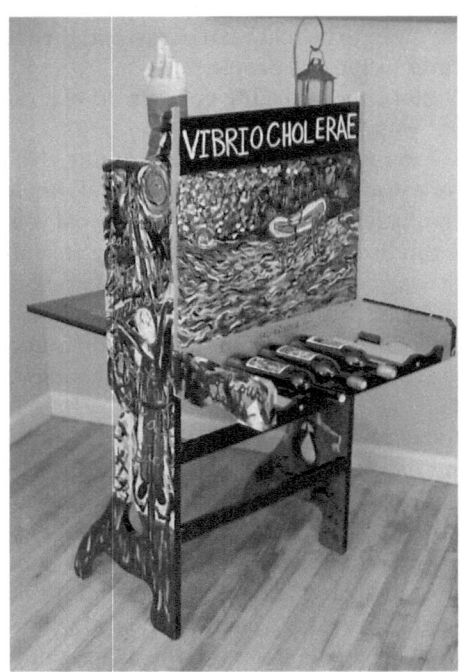

2013. Acrylic on old secretary

Panem et Circenses

The "Bread and Circuses" wine bar. 2013. An old secretary turned into a morality kiosk to display my politics and country wines. New York summers are a fruity lush paradise. The forager can feel all squire-like berry picking along the public road. With some vine yeast and modest initial investment in equipment, delicious, potent wines can be had by the time the five month lock down of a New York winter temporarily close all doors to hope, health and happiness.

Elderberry, dandelion, blueberry, and my personal favorite, blackberry. They are high proof, delusion of grandeur wines, aged just long enough to make the common man feel as powerful as any Governor* coached in the backseat of a black SUV.

First off, please note that it is an opinion piece. I am one of those rare modern fools who still preserves some quirky 19th century, human morals. Especially in matters of life and death. Winter, by virtue of the wine, recharge my dreams of equality, and I convince myself that, beyond communal law, no person has authority over another. That is, the Golden Rule should be the only indicator applied to all community problems—local, state, national, private, and public. Of course no democratic or totalitarian regimes ever abide by this simple application of human justice. And anarchism, which is likely impossible, is a label word reserved for the young and dumb, who might actually believe that such a system applied would preserve texting and orange juice for lunch when desired. On the other hand, localism is a word to scare the designer underwear off any crooked piece of garbage humanoid, who would suffer most under its auspices. That is, representatives of the multimillion billion dollar corporations—puppets easily placed into positions of power and influence. Our present day Governor* being one such corporito empowered by a system at war with the Golden Rule.

I sincerely believe in the libertarian idea of nullification, but only if backed up by a local economy. There are 19 million people living in this state. One Governor* and two parties, made up of many corrupt lawyers do not represent even the tiniest fraction of our families. They support ideas, loud ones, that seldom come from the hearts and minds of the real men and women who vote in November. Manufactured debates, wedge issues, to line up one candidate against the other, when both are just nefarious Party stooges snorting coke at private functions.

Which leads to one panel of the secretary with the following text: *The Farmer-governor Teaches the Coke-sniffing Governor° Empathy on a Stick*. My ancestor Enos Throop was Governor of New York State from 1829-1832. He was not re-elected because he was a farmer in a time when a farmer had to answer to each one of his farmer neighbors. His farmer neighbors did not want the Governor to tax them so that the farmers of Hamilton, Binghamton and Utica could have the state build a canal (the Chenango) to enrich their farms. Hence the interior of the secretary where I have Enos water board our present day Governor°. Why not? The President° declares that his minions at the CIA° have that right. So my imagination can too.

Another panel depicts the water-born disease of cholera, so often epidemic in 19th century America. Enos had to deal with the outbreak during his governorship, through no fault of his own. He traveled to inflicted towns and cities to oversee the tragedy and spread the idea of calm leadership throughout the panic. Cholera ruled the streets before Mr. Snow put the new science into practice, locally, without multimillion dollar profit driven research by GlaxoSmithKline°. The dandy choleras are out enjoying a Sunday evening stroll past the Broad Street pump.

On the back is a rack for the country wines, and a homage to the famous old west U.S. Marshal entitled *Leadership During the Time of the Cholera*.

Individual homemade country wines bear the following labels:

Dandelion toluene/a glass of golden sea/a cheap, if less efficient/ lobotomy
Blackberry—Ready or Not/V2O5/Try to keep your kids alive
Blueberry—Share this with a lover to woo/or a close friend to confide/ C5H8O2/or just glutaraldehyde
Elderberry Heaven/Elderberry Hell/offer Mr. Cuomo/ a glass of HCL

Finally the secretary's legs are dressed up with a skeletal Cuomo gesticulating with the words: "Andrew doth dance 'round the leukemic hole Jole".

And the Devil with, "Satan cries a toluene tear".

There is a human hand holding a salt loaf of bread, dried basil and tobacco strung around a piece of shale with a photograph of Cuomo and a painting of Throop pasted on a rock. I displayed the wine bar last spring and summer with an essay handout authored by yours truly, and an old speech by Governor Throop (that he wrote himself), explaining his position on the future construction of the Chenango Canal. Both are written by men bearing a conscience. A virtue that power brokers in the present day state of New York fear like rational people fear a family-shrinking infected water supply.

Come to the wine bar and we shall toast the nullification of corrupt human beings, which today means anyone seeking power as a representative in New York State.

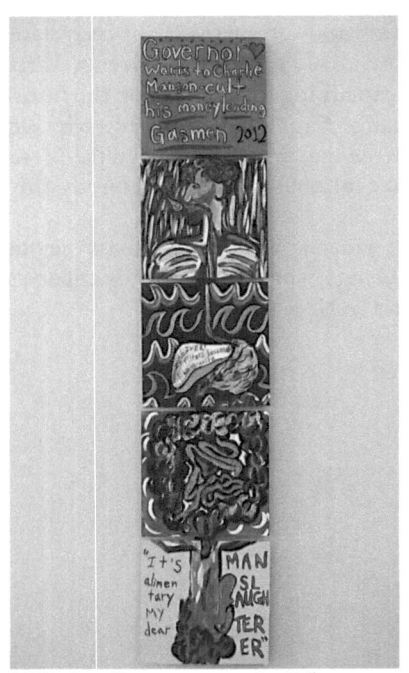

2012. Acrylic on canvas, 6 x 32"

It's Alimentary My Dear Manslaughterer

In with the bad, out with what used to be bad, but is better now than what stayed in. Proof that the Beatle's song "Helter Skelter" was bad medicine. Charles Manson took it in innocently enough, not knowing how it would mix things up inside, jive with his homicidal entitlement dreams, and be released into the wild. So he formed a cult and planned gruesome parties.

I believe that what makes a crazed Manson character must lie dormant in each and every one of us. We are guilty of abusing our own small powers sometimes. When power becomes absolute, whether expressed as micro from a stinky, run-down homicidal maniac's ranch in Los Angeles County, or macro, by the state mandate from a Mao Zedong or Andrew Cuomo, it will corrupt absolutely. We are familiar with the popular phrase. We repeat it at parties, yet at election time, still vote for either party in a one party-pretending to be two party-system. The one, true party is made up of the corporitos. They party all summer long on the private beaches of Lake Superior. In Oswego at late summer, one can witness their yacht captains battening down the hatches before a morning intercoastal departure to Florida. A month later they anchor their master's ships for many warm winter parties beneath Miami moons.

You wouldn't give Charles Manson the power to determine the potential fate of an entire people's water supply for profit. Even if it would employ all the violent LSD soaked hippies on earth. What has Andrew Cuomo written on his "saint" wall to have you assume that he is looking out for your best interests? Who is your state senator and assemblyperson? Are any of them hobbyist nutritionists, chemicals scientists, structural engineers, mothers and fathers who would struggle to afford a year's supply of home-delivered spring water?

The man in the painting knows the science. It's alimentary dear Watson. If you drink benzene, you suffer benzene. What might not be so obvious is that your representative in power would trade your physical well being for a small profit if a corporito told him to.

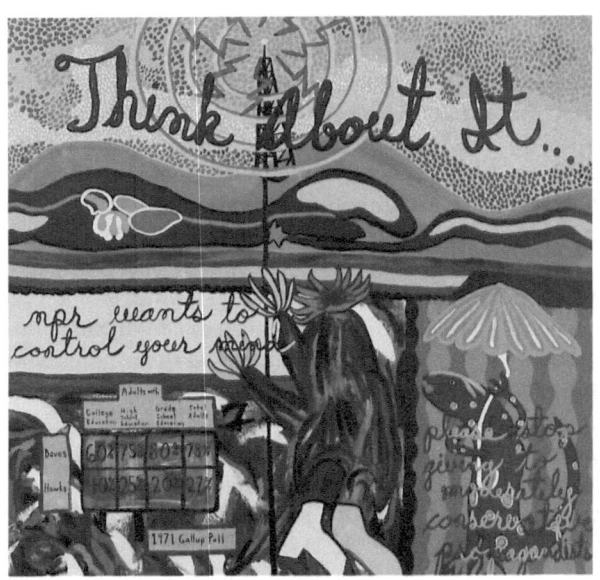

2015. Acrylic on canvas, 36 x 36"

Think About It

The fact that a 48 year old man, simple, shy and nearly as honest as his neighbor ever was, feels the need to take up what the elites of my state are claiming is a cause célebre over the pros and cons of chemically infecting our water supply, is a sign of the black SUV times.

Even our local "public" radio is in on the money game, selling advertising to the gas men who espouse child leukemia as a justifiable result of fake farmer Fred's purchase of a speed boat to play with while the subsidized high fructose corn syrup grows tall.

The governor is corrupt, his friends all greed punks, his girlfriend a very bad human being, and not even a good cook, really. Phenol crab cakes. A mixed green salad washed in naphthalene. A glass of formaldehyde Finger Lakes wine delivered to her door by the sleazy state senator who dreams paper money is happiness.

It amazes me that these lawyer-cowards are not hanging from a stick, by a thread, over a frack pool bubbling with mass community rage.

Stanley Milgram would have nodded his head while the people of the village turn the voltage up on their own screaming children.

So I take up paint and mix in what I think is the second most audacious power grab ever made by human beings. The first being the advent of probable nuclear annihilation by future lawyer-cowards. My neighbors watch and listen to the fake debate and wait to judge which side the hippies fall on. They all love CSN, and even Neil Young before he broke away and wrote the poetry of a grown-up. They just don't appreciate hippies bearing a conscience. All are waiting for the lawyer-cowards to set up the tent of the crazy circus debate on hydrofracking. And established tools like my local public radio people perpetuate the power grab with credit card payment glee. They don't need to be millionaires. They all just want to look like one.

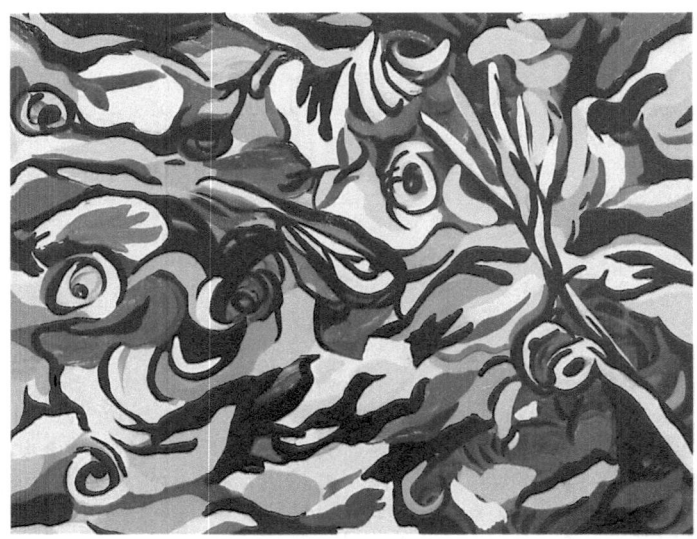

2014. Acrylic on canvas, 24 x 18"

Fissures Make Colorful Carcinogens, Yes?

A self-explanatory painting. Chemicals can be colorful. They are sent into the earth under high pressure. They come back up and float in a pool. That's the way the gas men want it to be understood. Innocuous, maybe even slightly normal, and downright grand if it provides jobs to the job hungry.

Atmospheric temperatures must have stabilized overnight. No longer news worthy. Nobody is talking about it. Huzzah! Tomorrows are purified for our progeny!

No, not really. But that is how the established 4th estate expects us to think.

Headlines from NPR would have us assume that global warming just stopped, and that summer's upstart is warm breeze and strawberries and wild fauna nesting soundly in the tall grass, swimming peacefully in pure and wild, wet waters, nibbling moist berries off the endless lush produce of mother earth...

NPR is government propaganda. Someone at the top of their machine is having lunch with Goebbels.

We could stop to get our bearings, reassess our dependencies, head into the future with strong backs and determination, but will not move a millimeter until our dollar takes its final nose dive into oblivion.

Still, with minimal effort we can break out of surface denial by making atmosphere talk our first attempt at every conversation. We could become mindful once again and use our cleanliness and good health and swell science to imitate 14th century Japanese royalty. We could write poetry, take day walks, stab to death the Carnegie Steel and Rockefeller Oil earth-hating drive-about we depend on more than our neighbors and families. We could naturalize our lives with creative job creation. That means we choose our local economies and dress them to our own survival tastes. Oil execs might have to be tortured gently. Fracking giants could have their heads politely lopped off. Military brass would get the picture after a sound fragging by its own sentient cannon fodder.

These punishing days will come. What's unbelievable is that the majority of intelligent human beings refuse to articulate this with any regular pattern.

Geeze, even without a blog to help clear her fuzzier dreams, the woolly mammoth got smitten with bright yellow buttercups still digesting.

So, carpe diem, verdad?

Yes, of course. But let's do it with some class. Let us witness some poetry crawl out of this Walmart funk hole we've born ourselves into. Use our liberal educations—read what the dead dogs wrote to become living lions once again. Don't let the consumer culture barons fool you any longer. The woolly mammoth was a blind consumer too. What was lost in non-acquisition of petroleum plastics, she made up for a thousand times by expressing her true nature.

Express your true nature. Become who you were before you were born. Focus your dreams toward creative survival. Yes, even with the weekly trade off of coins for Scott Tissue paper. Doom should be the only preoccupation of any species' grown-up. Even the crazed mega-neuronopolis doom of the human being king.

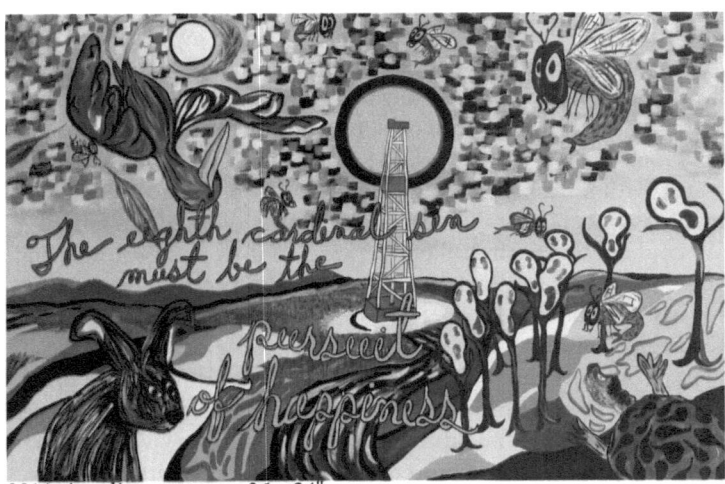

2014. Acrylic on canvas, 36 x 24"

The Eighth Cardinal Sin Must Be The Pursuit of Happiness

Finished a painting yesterday, a study in the human justification of "happiness and all else be damned". In the age of resources, it could be the great sin that fuels the other seven, and sadly, solely responsible for our final collapse. At least now I know why Jefferson declared it—so he could justify the Louisiana Purchase from a third party, own as many slaves as was necessary to seek happiness, and love make with the attractive ones whenever he got lonely from all that happiness finding.

Even well drillers just want to be happy. So do the anti-well drillers. The fracking protestor doesn't want a company from Texas feeding subterranean New York State with toxic juices. He jumps up and down with a sign and some friends, and drives his Mexican made Volkswagen 30 miles north back to his warm cozy Christmas house, heated dutifully by fracking labor in rural North Dakota. Likewise, families in Puebla appreciate the pesos generated from the Volkswagen Jetta-making plant, but hate the smell and the silver metal dust cutting into their kid's scalps. It's a trade-off for happiness. How else will they afford cable TV and French wine?

A boom economy in North Dakota keeps Lewis and Clark State Park lodge stocked to the rafters with bottled spring water from Maine. The recycling plant in Williston runs 24/7, and nowadays all residents are familiar with the new parts per million science, and therefore happier.

There is no human moral high ground in this debate. Even photovoltaics have to be made somewhere, out of unnatural, non-renewable things. Factories are never earth-friendly even when producing giant rectangular sun-catchers. We could live under a tree by the river, like Ratty in *The Wind in the Willows*, or all cozy tea-like at Mole End with the frack froth seeping up from the floorboards. Then we would pursue human happiness like rodentia in the wood, that is, with an amazing frack induced picnic luncheon of: "coldtonguecoldhamcoldbeefpickledgherkins-saladfrenchrollscresssandwidgespottedmeatgingerbeerlemonade-sodawater—"

"'O stop, stop,' cried Mole in ecstasies: 'This is too much!'

'Do you really think so?' inquired the Rat seriously 'It's only what I always take on these little excursions; and the other animals are always telling me that I'm a mean beast and cut it very fine!'"

Poor Kenneth Grahame was nervous about the future. No doubt he sniffed in the harsh, coal field stench of Nottinghamshire at some point in his life. Perhaps Toad was the pursuit of happiness amphibia incarnate. He was an ignorant spaz, buying up whatever was offered for immediate gratification, checking his many deeds off on the cardinal sin list, while thinking everyone else a simpleton. For it was only a matter of time before ratty, mole, and even cantankerous badger would want to race about the countryside in a newfangled automobile.

This painting shows nature finally joining those whom she cannot beat. I hate hydrofracking. I hate even more my pile of discarded packaging waiting to be recycled. A sack of oats and brown sugar would get the worst rat character through a hard winter. No need to drive over to the supermarket once a week for a 12 ounce box of already chewed Cheerios®. And any mole could tell you that the cooper would make a tub for the peanut butter if the cooper wasn't long ago executed by the always boy Peter Pan, henchman for ConAgra. We, the glorious anti-hydrofrackers have not yet learned how to stay put and buy in bulk. We think it's okay, this day-to-day world we participate in, as long as the water is as pure as our water factories can fake it like pros.

The poisonous web connects us all. I am sticking with my hypothesis—that we need to go all mid eighteenth century with access to antibiotics before catalysts like nuclear winter and cancer water make doom real without the hope of repair. Hence, follow through with my anti-fracking show in the spring. Keep the potable water flowing while pursuing our sickly happiness.

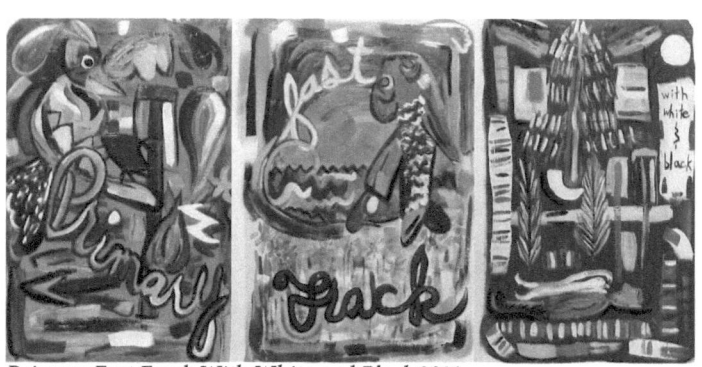

Primary Fast Frack With White and Black 2011.
(3)Acrylic on canvas, 27 x 15"

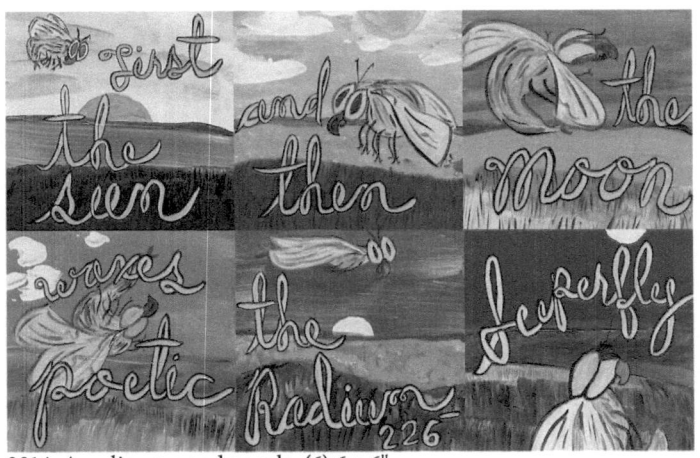

2014. Acrylic on wood panels, (6) 6 x 6"

First the Sun and Then the Moon Waxes Poetic The Radium-266 Superfly

I learn something new each time I research the side effects of hydrofracking:
http://www.counterpunch.org/2012/11/09/fracking-and-radioactivity/
Radium-266 is bad for humans, but inspiring beyond words to its namesake mutant species "superfly". All day and night the superfly sings lustily of days to come and gone by—the willow that stretched to the stars and cracked with the first big wind, the last squirrel to pack soil over a nut, pick its head up to the sun, and cough up a blood clot, the dreams of a mate to fly with over the lake counting the floating fish in the moonlight... The superfly is a poet and a visionary. He sleeps subterranean for seven years subsisting in a bath of charged radium ions. Then at pre-dawn on midsummer night he rises with the sun to sing the song of the world and find a mate to cuddle up with for the next long radioactive sleep.

It wasn't enough to have a hundred toxic chemicals bubbling in a murky frack pool, so we opted for mining some well-known carcinogenics too.

With a three-year lease, Landowner Ted can now afford an F350 run on natural gas, a tiller with its own choke, and cash payments for his grandson's chemotherapy.

Also, unfortunately, for the next 16,000 years, Landowner Ted's descendants cannot step outside without a mosquito netting cage. The superflies' bite is instant death, and no pesticide can kill it.

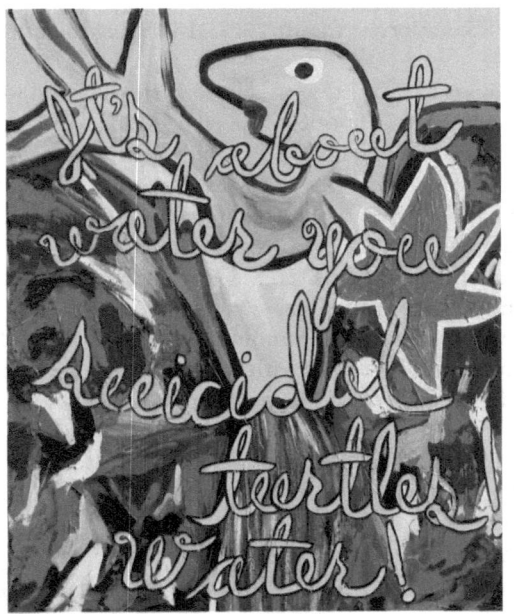

2015. Acrylic on canvas, 16 x 20"

It's About Water You Suicidal Turtles! Water!

Opening night in Hamilton is over. I am freed up to continue amassing the first local environment painting exhibition that will be the last ever necessary. All adults of earth shall pass through the gallery thinking, "What has happened?" and "Why was I not meditating like an old ghost after having babies and teaching them the Golden Rule?"

I am convinced that, in the West anyway, art and artist must become the moral bullhorn to check humanity's penchant for cardinal sin. I remember back during the Iraq "war" when I wrote to 40 local ministers and priests chastising them for being scared little puppies to their congregations. It seemed not one of them had the guts to outwardly protest the slaughter. The SUV's kept driving in on Sunday mornings to hear of their personal greatness—the holy men had bills to pay, bell towers to repair at exorbitant union wages. Either way, protest or not, there would be many more crimes committed by the lost sheep, so keep quiet and share the spoils. I scolded them with the knowledge of how the church became the Hummer became the church. Not one response. Of course I never supplied a return address (I was an artist not a prophet).

Environmental disaster, like war, is not a concern to the corporate God men and women. Heaven is hard work. Few have time to think about earth, water, and air anymore. A good economy will refurbish the church, and while so many are frantically busy applying themselves to bloating the coffers (by all means), little artists paint pictures hand-slapping the bad men. Even priests!

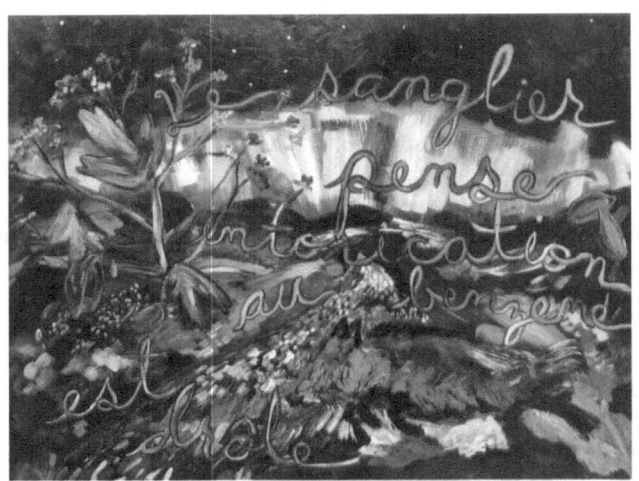

The Boar Thinks Benzene Poisoning Is Funny 2012.
Acrylic on canvas, 18 x 14"

France Paintings

These paintings were made during a brief residency in South-western France. There was a sixth, a trout "swimming joyfully in a pool of toluene paint thinner", that was bought last year at a show in Cooperstown. In America a purchaser of a trout can be a fish lover and a gas drilling supporter at the same time. Here it is not necessary to connect art with conscience. Hence the ridiculous Croesus wealth-building of perverts like Jeff Koons and Lady Gaga.

I do not speak or write in the French language. These translations are pathetic, but that's okay because the fauna of France do not speak French either. But they are inclined to chew off our arms for the audacious move by the bad (rotten) apples among us who are encroaching upon *their* property rights.

These paintings and more aim to stop the hydrofracking industry from invading our beautiful upstate New York countryside. A tough front to form indeed. My local public radio station, WRVO, at the behest of fracking millionaires, is telling us to "think about it". That is, accept the reality that propaganda is king, even among our supposed publicly funded institutions.

I had a nice time painting in France. For eight days I was hounded by an angry ghost in a 13th century bastide. It was late October and it drove me to bed down in the unheated studio. To be polite I told my hostess that I was keeping myself in a restless state to stimulate creativity. No. I was terrified, painting every waking moment while watching my back. Beside a farmer's field, I took one long walk on a Roman road, and visited a castle on the last day.

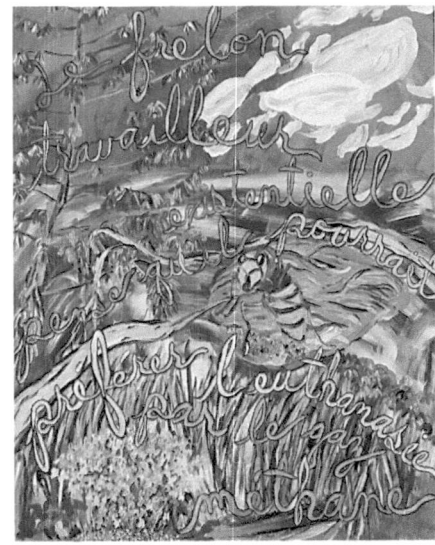

The Existential Worker Hornet Thinks It Might Prefer Euthanasia By Methane Gas 2012.
Acrylic on canvas, 14 x 18"

The Trout Swims Joyfully in a River Pool of Toluene Paint Thinner 2012.
Acrylic on canvas, 14 x 18"

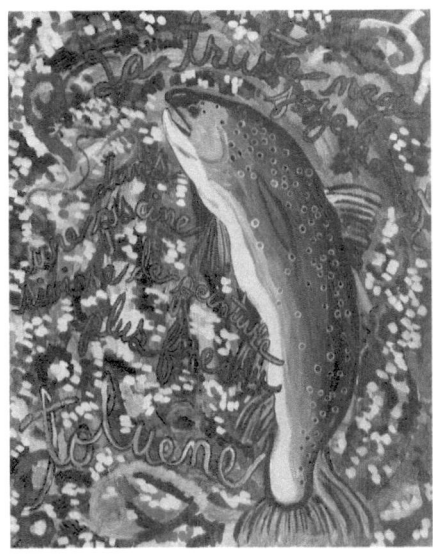

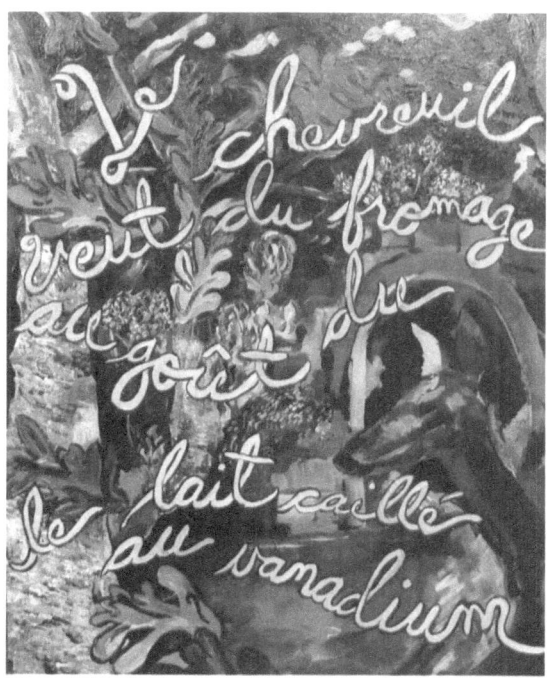

The Roe Deer Wants Cheese To Taste Like Vanadium Curd 2012. Acrylic on canvas, 14 x 18"

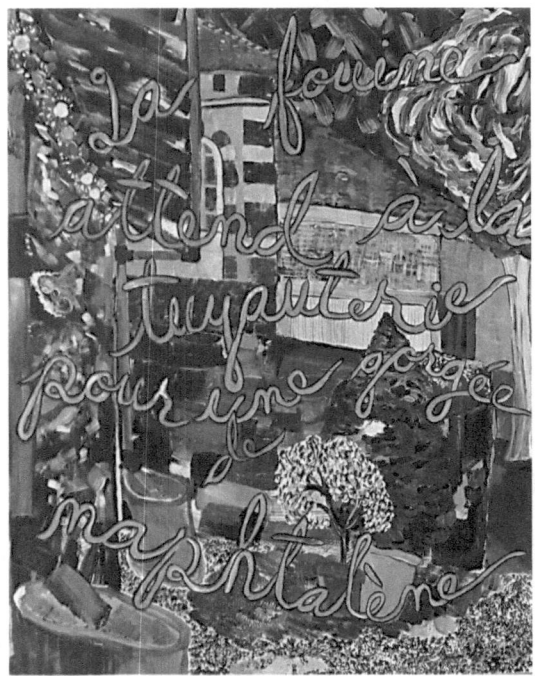

The Stone Marten Waits at the Pipe Fitting For a Sip of Naphthalene 2012. Acrylic on canvas, 14 x 18"

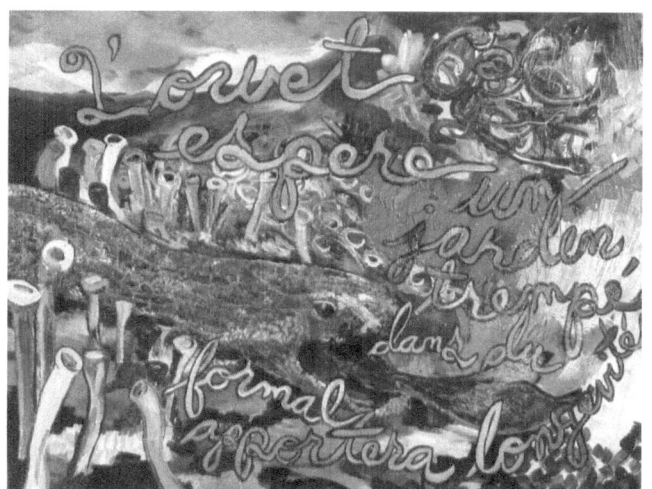

*The Slow Worm Hopes a Garden Soaked in Formaldehyde Will
Bring Longevity* 2012. Acrylic on canvas, 18 x 14"

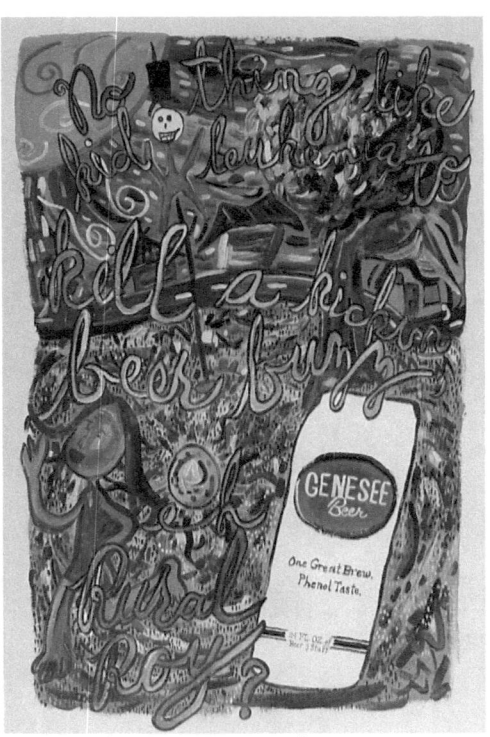

2011. Acrylic on paper, 15 x 22"

No Thing Like Kid Leukemia to Kill a Kickin' Beer Buzz, Eh Rural Roy?

More often than not, I don't think people do the right thing for their children, nieces, nephews, second cousins, etc. We like to think that we do, but no, not really. For instance, every time we let a child into a car, and forgo the crash helmet, we have given up the right to proclaim we always have their best safety in mind. It's easy to pretend that Johnny and Sue look cool and comfortable in a carpeted projectile set at a cruising speed of 70 mph, among a hundred other luxury projectiles. However, the science is clear. A kid with a crash helmet on will survive more accidents than one without. Likewise, just making a concerted effort to avoid unnecessary trips to the mall, or pediatrician who, because insurance companies told her to, refuses to come to your child's bedside when the latter is exhausted with double pneumonia. Similarly, car manufacturers could be mandated to fit all automobiles with steel roll cages. 77% less fatalities on the road coupled with helmet wearing required by law. We could have the safest highways on earth by next year with laws passed for the betterment of society and not the institutional sleazy squeeze off overhead to make a profit.

This is how I often see the good and bad of the world—through the eyes of an omnipotent care provider. I wish I had the ultimate safety control over earth's children. Who wouldn't? War would end. Nuclear weapons would be dismantled and stuffed back up the crack of any nation's nincompoop stronghold that ever thought having them was a bright idea. Pharmaceutical companies would no longer need the lure of Croesus profit to discover helpful medicines; men and women of science would have the highest honor among populations, and not need to be told by a greedy death administrator where to focus their attention. The successes of agronomists would be awarded at ceremonies broadcast prime time. For Christ's sake, they fed the world didn't they? Beats having a public sex change on TV. NASA would be stripped of all its Luke Skywalker Star Wars machines, and fitted with new admirable words to replace the most wasteful acronym in the history of mankind. *National Altruistic Scientists Association*, or something like that, and the moon remains a lit up dead thing to look at in the night sky. Finally, I would give companies like Exxon-Mobil and Range Resources thirty days to discover and implement renewable alternative energy makers under the threat of cutting each member of their board of directors (and all their unhelmeted limo drivers) in half.

Ho hum. Just wistful dreaming.

The girl in the painting is green from vanadium splashes as she dances through the sprinkler atop the Marcellus Shale on a hot summer day. Her Dad sold Range Resources the right to douse her with carcinogens, because he was told by a qualified spokesperson with no scientific research skills that fracking was safe, don't worry, here's a hundred grand. Dad was glad. Paid off the mortgage and the truck. The money got spent, and most unfortunately, his daughter's natural bone development too.

All that fast money joy, and now this downer? Buzz kill! Oh well, nothing he can do about it now except move.

"For Christ's sake, Suzy, leave the damn helmet in the yard! Get in the car. We gots to go!"

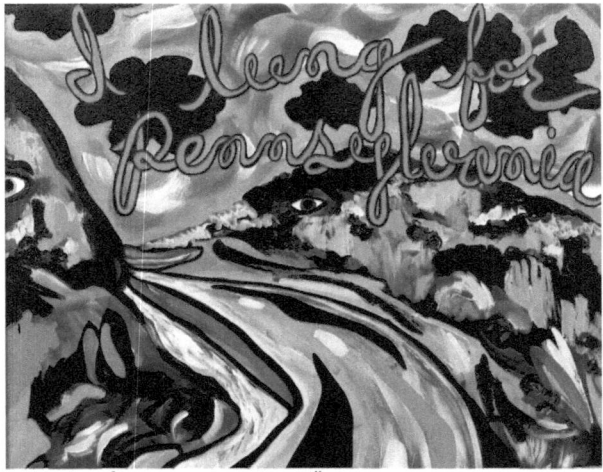

2015. Acrylic on canvas, 18 x 14"

I Lung For Pennsylvania

As the calls to frack intensify worldwide, I feel hoodwinked to a posture of silly for entitling this exhibition *Capillary Reaction: Hyrdofracking and Irrevocable Loss*. I remember my wife and I sitting in the brown window chairs brainstorming an idea the morning after the ArtRage gallery director asked me to come up with a title to the show. Sure, it's a good one to teach a lesson about toxicity and parts per million, how just a little chemical goes a long way in a glass of ice water. It is good to know about the half-lives of radioactive elements—20,000 years is a long time to be a carcinogen. I think everyone gets the science. Documentary's like *Gasland* and *Gasland 2* provide a basic scientific overview of "what if?" And no sane person will lie to another with the claim, "Benzene is harmless, here let me drink a gallon straight to prove it". We are told that the industry is not mandated to list the chemicals used in the process, but some are known. For instance, toluene. No one debates its use in hydrofracking. Here is what science says about it (from EPA chemfact sheet 1994):

Repeatedly breathing large amounts of toluene, such as when "sniffing" glue or paint, can cause permanent brain damage. As a result, humans can develop problems with speech, hearing, and vision. Humans can also experience loss of muscle control, loss of memory, and decreased mental ability. Exposure to toluene can also adversely affect the kidneys. Laboratory animal studies and, in some cases, human exposure studies show that repeat exposure to large amounts of toluene during pregnancy can adversely affect the developing fetus. Other studies show that repeat exposure to large amounts of toluene adversely affects the nervous system, the kidneys, and the liver of animals.

In *Gasland 2* we also learn a little bit about civil engineering. A typical frack well is encased for protection by an inch of cement, and if groundwater is never to be compromised, this wittle-bitty cement lining cannot crack until the end of time. *Capillary Reaction: Hydrofracking and Irrevocable Loss* point made. End of debate. End of story. Well is broke, chemicals leak into water supply, ecological disaster creeps up all over the country. We get it. Capillaries—streams, tributaries, rivers, the sea! A moral to the science story: Hydrofracking is bad for your health. So are nuclear weapons. Everyone knew radioactive fallout was bad, but Eisenhower and Kennedy still went ahead with thermonuclear detonation celebrations in the atmosphere. Why did my parents and grandparents duck under their desks and beds like frightened puppies? What made them cower for something that need not have been inevitable?

For an answer, I shall rename the title to the exhibition. I should have sent this one instead, but at the time I didn't fully develop my artistic hypothesis. Basically I intend to prove that the people in power, real power, do not work for the common welfare. They represent the darker side in the duality of human nature. They are bad men and women.

Here's the new title:

Pigs at the Trough: Hydrofracking and the Greed Mash That Squeals Cash

Positions of power held in the U.S. are heavily lopsided towards attracting bad people. A good one or two can sneak in, but most are bad, driven by low human qualities, such as avarice, greed, pride, etc... We all know someone close who is admired by others in our family or community for being, calm, rational, kind, and selfless to a degree that he or she would make a very good leader. But for some reason, these people never end up in politics. Why is that? Well, for starters... They are humble, just, and seeking a life of fulfillment which might include a little bit of wisdom building along the way. They shun politics. It is bad for their humanity.

The potential harmful effects of Hydrofracking are not a subject for debate any more than the potential harm an asteroid the size of Guam would cause to denizens of the earth after impact.

Okay. So the low among us, with the help of a very lazy, profit driven media, steer the debate away from reality. Politicians from fracking states will say "Aw, what a bunch of killjob scientists. Anyway, it's just not true!" They will tell the lie because they are bribe-sniffing, dirty rotten human beings of the lowest order. And the media houses like Fox TV and MSNBC will repeat the lie because they are owned by bribe-sniffing, dirty rotten human beings of the lowest order. Do not for an instant think that New

York State is free of very bad men and women. Our two senators, just by virtue of their senatorostorship alone, as prerequisite to this high job in a federal oligarchy, sold out to the highest bidder long ago. Both Schumer and Gillibrand side with the winners. Katko actually used hydrofracking to campaign with the repeated lie, "It'll bring jobs and it's safe". Fox did the leg work. People who think they are conservative, but are really just effective television watchers, heard of the "debate", did not get information about potential rise in leukemia rates, and voted in the majority for a bribe-sniffing, dirty rotten human being of the lowest order. But no worries, Maffei was and is one too. No different at our state level. Cuomo need not care what the voter thinks because no one votes philosophically anymore. New York votes party, and both parties are overrun by bribe-sniffing, dirty rotten human beings of the lowest order. In a perfect vacuum, when asked about the environment, there is not one adult alive besides psychopath, who would deny the hope of the cleanest air, water and soil for his children and children's children. However, the debate gets spun, the words "jobs" and "economy" pop up over and over in rapid media succession, and the great debate on human health is manufactured and maintained by the quintessence of avarice in the flesh—our "representatives". At the last gubernatorial election, who in the two-party system debated clean air? Clean water? Healthy soil? Was there just one informational meeting on how best to steward the environment? Yet all constituents care about their air. All voters want good health.

Dear reader, know thy pigs at the trough. The only participation one should have with a high elected leader today, is shame heckling.

I Lung For Pennsylvania is my Milton Glaser design for promoting Keystone state anti-tourism in the future. It should remind everyone to stay the hell away from all Pennsylvania has to offer. Also, know this my fellow New Yorkers. As long as you keep voting for criminals, you will get exactly what you deserve. Your next corporate governor will sell your state to the highest bidder in the room. Count on it.

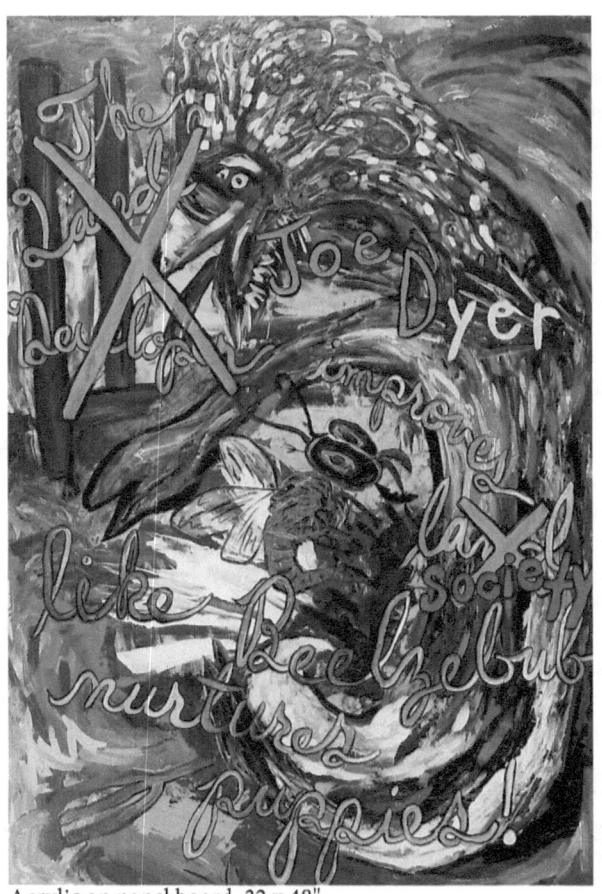

Acrylic on panel board, 32 x 48"

The Joe Dyer Improves Society Like Beelzebub Nurtures Puppies!

Joe Dyer is running for State Senate * in the 37th district of New York State. My friend Pat called me up yesterday to say so. He read Joe's biography while I sat in a brown chair, my mind spinning into overdrive, contacting memory, learning, and philosophy to process the new, personally pertinent information. Joe was our peer all through elementary and high school. He was a dandy, and a mean one at that. I believe the word "preppie" came into use during eighth grade. A preppie would be likened to a "soc" from the book *The Outsiders*, still assigned reading for kids today, as if there are no contemporary teen fiction authors worth their salt, and its author S.E. Hinton is some kind of generation leaping teen guru of eternal wisdom.

Though tall and long-armed, Joe was no physical in-your-face bully. But he was mean. Disdainful. Stuck-up was the term to designate elitist young people back then. Joe was an effeminate young boy, which confused many of the other kids, but at that tender age, not enough to turn their confusion into cruelty. Our families all had more or less an equal amount of disposable income, so other, more finesse, status lines were drawn. The preppie click started young, fourth grade in my school. It was all due mainly to geography and dress. Joe hung around with the girls of the same development. There was money in these houses, not a great deal more than the rest of town, but enough to improve upon the kid's wardrobes. Joe and his girl friends had the latest from Izod®, Levi's®, and the ever-cool sounding OshKosh B'gosh®. They sported a high fashion that all the kids coveted but most were unable to acquire by the fifth grade.

Salvatore was a friend of mine, who had recently moved into a big house in Joe's development. For a stretch of several months I went over to his house most days after school. We practiced disco in Sal's living room and walked around the development pretending to be fifth grade cool. Often Joe would be out with his gaggle of well-dressed girls taunting Sal with the mean kid slang of the time like, "Why are you hangin' out with gay-boy Throop? He's a fag—Tell him to go home." To Sal's credit, he always defended me. Sal didn't think I was gay. Neither did I. Who knew what homosexual was anyway? I may not have been gay, but I was definitely a romantic. In school I sent Lisa, one of Joe's girl friends, a carnation on Valentine's Day. She wasn't ready to be loved, at least not by me, and so defensively called me a gayboy in reaction to the flower gift, which was unfortunate because of her position as trend-setter at our elementary school. Joe, Lisa, and the girl friends shared their prejudice to other preppie boys and girls, and together they fashioned quite a scary hell out of my elementary school experience.

Joe Dyer remained a condescending peer throughout the rest of our hometown school years. As I recall, by graduation, beyond being an impeccable dresser, he never stood out in any way but average. According to his biography he went to Georgetown University for his bachelor's degree, and received a Master's in International Affairs from Columbia University.

Here is some Joe Dyer professional life story straight from his Senate® campaign Facebook®:

As Senior Vice President of Global Policy for Visa, Inc.®, Joe launched the strategy to open the China market for American financial companies, which became a landmark case at the World Trade Organization (WTO)® that the U.S. won. For over a decade at AIG®, he served as a Director of Corporate and International Affairs where he worked hard to open foreign markets to U.S. goods and services. This helped create good jobs back in America.

Joe was then appointed to serve as a Senior Advisor and Chief of Staff to the Under-Secretary for Domestic Finance in the U.S. Department of Treasury® from 2003 to 2005. He returned to AIG® in 2007 and planned to spend the rest of his career there focused on expanding business in international markets. But, like many regular employees, he lost his job during the financial crisis and was left with only his personal integrity, resolve and entrepreneurial spirit to provide for his family in the highest taxed county in the nation. He learned how losing nearly everything can sometimes provide you with even more, if one is willing to work hard and pursue the American Dream.

And finally, the reason why Joe is running for office, according to the little lying satan perched on his left shoulder:

Joe Dyer is running for New York State Senate * *to bring the voice of regular, hard-working families back to Westchester. He knows what it means to balance a budget, hold the line on spending and create jobs by opening new markets for American products.*

A veritable saint of a man, Joe Dyer.

That should be enough about Joe for me to leave his memory the heck alone. But I am feeling a bit feral today. Wild in many ways not akin to Joe, but in the sense of unbelievable why and mega-stupendous how. How can Americans be so politically and philosophically drained of even a drop of reactionary dignity? Why is Joe, the stuck-up nothing special preppie of my memory poised to have influential power in state politics as well as the wealth and status of Croesus? The people of Joe's über taxed county have a choice between two candidates to represent them this November, and one of them was high up in a company that took nearly a tenth of a trillion dollars of tax payer money in a bailout. A couple weeks later the candidate may have been spotted at The St. Regis Resort in Monarch Beach, California enjoying a half a million dollar spa vacation with other jolly, upbeat executives. And if he wasn't there in person, in spirit he was more responsible than anyone else in his district for the financial crisis of 2008.

So many darting reactions to Joe's social success. I need to take hold of one and fly with it.

In my artistic, fatherly, husbandly, morally, joyfully non-humble opinion, I believe Joe Dyer to be the scourge of the earth, the antithesis of good, a representative of King Beelzebub if anyone anywhere still actually believed in the domain of Hell. Joe is my spiritual enemy because to a sensitive painter and poor man he can be nothing else. What he sees as accomplishment, I have spent a lifetime countering, for I sincerely believe that his achievements stand up as the earth's only evil. Joe Dyer is avarice incarnate. In my little world of control, the means always justify the ends; one reaps what one sows, etc. Privately, Joe will get his just desserts someday, but in the mean time—Oh, in the mean time!

I am working on an exhibition of my paintings protesting the probable arrival of the natural gas industry to upstate New York. I am not getting paid. My wife and I are investing in all the materials and time necessary to express my deep concern for the future of our water supply. Joe Dyer, if insanely elected, and if ready to tow his parties' line, could be the deciding vote to lift the present moratorium and clear a path to the monster nature-haters. This fracking hoard will make their millions, while laundering a piece of profit back to Joe and his cronies, under the guise of improving the economy for simpleton Jack the corn farmer. And then when the fissures crack, and all the gas has risen, and the pools have brought childhood leukemia to the gay boys and girls of his grand-children's childhood, Joe Dyer will have been long since dead, laid to rest some time ago with the rich man's understanding that there is no retributive justice for the people ever. Joe Dyer must envy me much more than I want his money. He knows he makes nothing but trickle-down sorrow for so many people of the earth. He must know too, privately, that his money and power is not self-made. For Joe Dyer it was all luck, placement, and yes, hard work, but toward nothing, nothing, nothing of eternal merit. There are only so many hours in a week, and for Joe Dyer to resumé such a life means he neglected all the life wonders that I hold dear to my heart. If he is as good a father as I, a better husband, a gentler soul, then let the earth ram its pin-hole into the sun, for I must be a crazed lunatic.

Americans suffer from a live and let live psychosis. It must be evolutionary, from a time way back when we had to subsist in small clans for survival, and we trusted, intuitively, all charac-ters of the tribe. If Joe Dyer was to gain business respect in 8,000 B.C.E., he would have to be one of the best wampum stringers, for he certainly could not come of age as a warrior or wise man. And, since wealth was shared by all, the chief would have ordered his banishment the moment Joe wove his first Izod® alligator mocca-sins. Individual status was achieved with reason and consent of the tribe, not acquired through billion dollar bureaucratic contracts or their equivalent, which at that time of course, did not exist.

That constituents of the 37th district of New York will even step out of their cars to vote for Joe Dyer, and not blow up the poll-ing station for the fascist insult made to their children and their children's children by the initial placement of Joe, is how I can tell that this crackpot civilization is finally kaput.

When executives of British Petroleum®, via Halliburton® negli-gence, kill eleven people on an oil rig, while choking the life of the gulf of Mexico and beyond for millennia to come, and yet not one Joe Dyer dandy among them spends an overnight in a Mississippi county jail cell, then the race has finally achieved an evolutionary reverse-jump. It is on a moral leap back to monkeydom.

Just a couple years before that tragedy, powerful friends helped their monetary equals at AIG® to the American till for 85 billion dollars, a sum that distributed responsibly could do a positive good for the nation, perhaps end homelessness or supply age care to all grandparents in need. Yet no storming of the Bastille ensued. Not a peep from the masses. Not one justice stoning of any Joe Dyer involved.

Today my moral adversary runs for state office on the Republican® ticket claiming the desire to represent hard working Westchester County families, even after public knowledge that his darling institutions are directly responsible for the high taxes they pay. It is such a tall irony that it has broke my mind into the realm of the silly-absurd.

Joe Dyer is not a good man. He is a bad man. Not because he is rich but because he is rich. He is a liar. He does not wish to represent working families. He wants to enslave working families on his international financial plantation of woe because it means a purchase of a yacht for him. I hate Joe Dyer and despise his society because it has become a topsy-turvy world of anti-justice for the many, and manipulation of all wealth and power toward the central class. You are all gay boys and girls to Joe Dyer. You are below him. He believes success is directly proportional to wealth acquisition. Fortunately, this belief can only evolve into a parasite infecting the entire culture if we believe it too.

Unfortunately, a broad majority do.

Yes, like Jimmy Cliff, even the poor poet-painter wants his share of what's his. But he will never get it, and justly so, if he thinks good of what Joe Dyer's got. After over twenty years privately observing the human comedy, Ron Throop has come to the conclusion that great wealth can only come to the average, the predictable, the steady and of course, the corrupt. Joe represents a new species classified by Linnaean Taxonomy, and will pass on its characteristics to his unlucky progeny. Let me see if I can get this right. Joe is progenitor to *homo smiling scumbagus*, an up and coming species of Armageddon.

Dear Joe Dyer, contemporary public figure of my condemned youth, I wish you continued success on your neo-con psychopath of the über-rich. My only regret in this memory of you is that I did not split your lip when we were small.

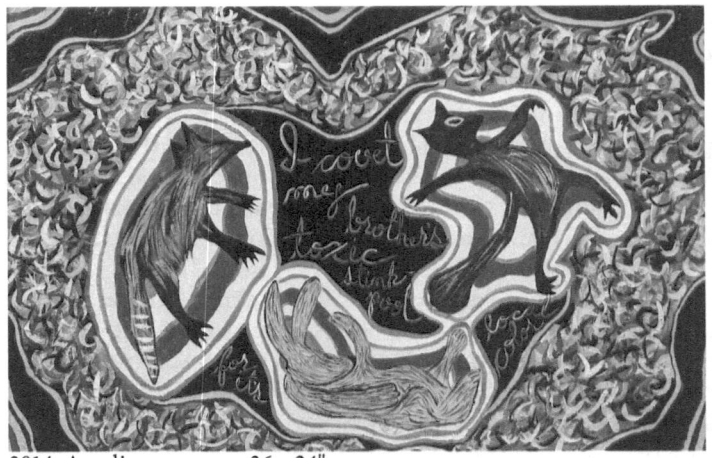

2014. Acrylic on canvas, 36 x 24"

I Covet My Brother's Toxic Stink Pool For It's Local Color

One morning these unlucky animals ventured near the frack pool for a drink. Raccoon knew something was wrong when he · peered across the liquid stink and saw rabbit turning pink. Moments later the three were asphyxiated and fell into the pool, dead.

Now I don't know about you reader, but I am bowled over with envy at the man who can get ahead by leasing land that will remain his until it gets sold, or as long as legacy can hold out. Property rights once temporarily shared for hunting, or leasing fields to a farmer to grow experimental soy and corn, now can provide a potent chemical pool to all and sundry. A good neighbor won't be so greedy. Maybe he'll invite the local children over for a dip on a hot day. He already made his money. Anyway, it's safe as certain, and their collective pee, no matter how acidic, won't dilute the deadly levels of toluene unless the kids were presoaked for several days in 55 gallon drums of Kentucky bourbon.

When I found out my brother built one of these pools, I was so jealous of his country living. He always seemed to be one up on his city mouse sibling. He got to kill deer and eviscerate them on the ground. He got a big diesel pick up truck. He got to ride a green tractor around the property, and say words like "wood lot" and "water well". He used to boast about the latter whenever his family came over for dinner. He said our water tasted like swimming pool, and he'd get all proud about his purer supply, and start bragging about the strawberry patch and vegetable garden, on and on about how good irrigation ditches made big fat watermelons grow.

Of course that all ended the morning the results came back from oncology, and it turned out his whole family and the dog had cancer.

I still envy his pool. It has a sweet smell. It never freezes over, even in February, and the crystal colors on the surface shimmer all rainbowy.

Now for a serious talk about Ron Paul, libertarianism, and property rights, and how to apply these concepts to hydrofracking. I have a weak spot for Ron Raul, the twelve term congressman from Texas who ran for President three times, once as a libertarian, and twice on the Republican ticket. He is a thinker, more of a philosopher than a politician. Even if his philosophy could be challenged in healthy debate, I voted for him in the last election because he was the only candidate available who was not a disgusting human being. Lobbyists always stayed clear of his office on Capitol Hill. He believed like Jefferson "that government is best that governs least". Money in government, according to Paul, is the bane of modern society, in that there will always be tremendous winners and losers. In our present day, the winners representing the military, medical, educational, industrial complex, and the losers being everyone else, divided into warring factions, all pining for their teeny-weeny sliver slice of the government pie.

Through Paul I realized that I have always been of a similar philosophy, more or less. That is, I am a libertarian who believes strongly in the Golden Rule. I use it as an individual, more so than a political philosophy. That is, I am a moralist in theory, but practical enough to never apply it seriously to others, and expect good results. Because...

"Preacher was talkin'
    There's a sermon he gave.
    He said, 'Every man's conscience
    Is vile and depraved'"

—Bob Dylan from "Man in a Long Black Coat"

Enter the concept of property rights, a basis of libertarian philosophy, and an example of cheap lip service paid by the Republicans and Conservatives of my country. Basically it means that you and I as individuals, through rights of property, whether that property exists as owning land, or just owning the rights to ourselves, should in theory have more power than all groups or governments that lobby and/or make laws. Individual rights trump group rights always, as long as no one else suffers from an individual's actions. Property rights only work if courts invoke and society enforces them equally for all.

So, according to Ron Paul and libertarians, if you own a piece of land, not only should you be free from paying property taxes, but you can do with the land whatever you please, as long as you're not infringing on the property rights of your neighbor. So again in theory, libertarians will tell you Monsanto is criminal because it's pollen escapes boundaries and destroys the individual farmer's seed crop. However, a guy selling seeds on his own land has every right to do so, without local, state, or federal government regulation, so long as his seeds do not hurt anyone.

In an interview last year, Paul was asked what he thought about hydrofracking. True to his form, he applied libertarian philosophy to the controversy. He thought out loud for the interviewer and came to a decision. First, he noted that if there is a strong potential to infect the groundwater that others connect to, then hydrofracking should be outlawed. Then, after further thought, he admitted that just the actual process defies a libertarian point-of-view. Hydraulic fracturing runs horizontal, across boundaries. It crosses properties below. So if Fred has a well, and the well shoots toxic chemicals sideways, then his neighbors Bob and Tom lose their individual right to keep their property free from toxic chemical invasion. From another angle (my own) it could be said that gas companies would be liable to pay Bob and Tom for use of the property a mile below their feet, which of course, would make such a venture impossible to profit by.

It's true, after the well is drilled, hydrofracking ignores the property rights of everybody else affected, whether that be from potential health risks to the individual, or loss of compensation from unauthorized land lease below ground.

Republicans and conservatives are lying to themselves about hydrofracking if they also subscribe to the concept of individual property rights. Now again, in theory, if they allow a legislative body (the state) to determine if hydrofracking will be allowed, then might it be that the Republicans and Conservatives are so in name only, yet may actually lean more toward a philosophy of socialism, or even a light totalitarianism/fascism?

I think so.

A quick note about libertarian philosophy. It cannot work beyond the political machinations of a clan type of government. Property rights for individuals are not, nor have ever been universally applied in the history of civilization. But it can act as a very good justice indicator. Applied to hydrofracking, one can easily prove to a Republican or Conservative brother-in-law that his philosophy is just made up of re-hashings of Fox News diatribes mixed in with a hot shot of greed and entitlement.

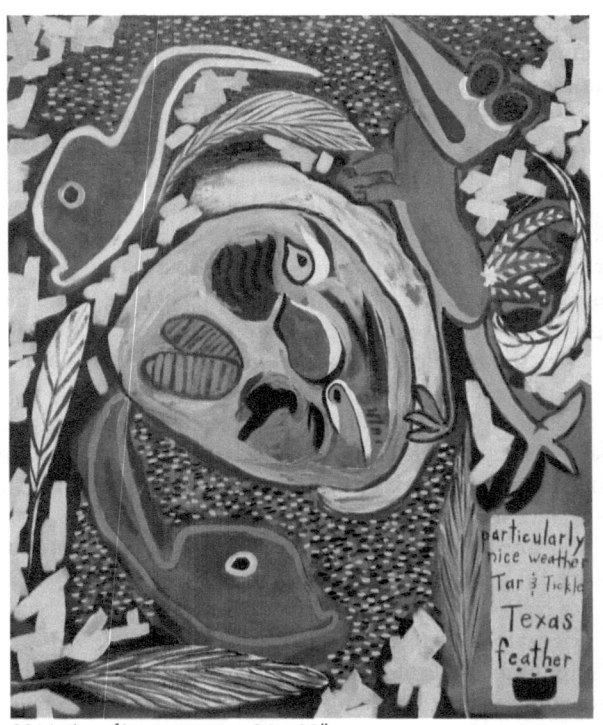

2014. Acrylic on canvas, 24 x 30"

Particularly Nice Weather, Tar and Tickle Texas Feather

While at the periodontist yesterday I read a recent interview with
Bob Dylan in AARP magazine. Rotting gums, Bob Dylan, and
a bland publication representing a powerful lobby of 35 million
members. Not much excitement to look forward to after 50, if I
decide to tow the line with this lifestyle. Anyway, Dylan remarked
that he is no longer passionate, that that's a young man's game.
The elders should seek wisdom, or at least shut-up and fake it
with boring silence. Yet in the same interview he admitted that
perhaps there isn't a generational difference between the minds
of old and young after all. Maybe grandpa can relate to all things
granddaughter and vice-versa. Then he told the interviewer that
he doesn't worry if his records sell or not. His business people take
care of that.

Here is a point in time where both wisdom and passion can col-
laborate, if one chooses to act, whether she be fifteen or fifty-five.
First the facts up front. Bob Dylan is a multimillionaire who has a
business team of professionals working for him night and day. The
AARP is a multimillion dollar lobby putting all American people
over 50 in a blender and aging them together on high puree. A
periodonist is expensive but worth the investment if you still long
for a kiss at midnight, but hope to avoid your lover's tongue prying
off your lower partial.

Period.

Now I will spend a moment in my imagination, and work
through the institutional obfuscations that plague all innocent
ninety-nine percenters of the earth, and leave them daily worried,
bewildered, and confused. The media has never been so practi-
cally omnipotent wielding its power to keep minds, and what are
supposed to be wiser minds (those over 50 at the periodontist), at
rest, in a kind of living death-rest way. I read what Bob Dylan has
to say, and suddenly feel, that yeah, maybe he's right. I shouldn't
be passionate anymore. I should just grow old, find drugs to de-
crease my joint pain, and shut up. Even if I arrived to the periodonist singing along and imagination dancing to what Jagger and
Richards thought passionate back in 1974, I must come to terms
with my old age eventually, give up all firecracker electricity in
my veins, get out of the car, check my belt, adjust my glasses, and

enter one of the many waiting rooms of my future. No spark. No passion. Just quiet wisdom. And look! The new issue of AARP. Advertisements, pop culture, television, an interesting hobby, travel, gum disease, tooth extraction, and then death. Many studies have proven that the dispassionate actually choose what type of deodorant to buy. The dispassionate want quick weeknight meals, packages to tropical island getaways, historical vignettes, and even an interview with an elder, creative millionaire who, at present, is pretending to be a 1940's lounge crooner.

Sometimes my mind can work through these persistent media distortions. I actually agreed with Bob Dylan, until I got back into my car, turned on the CD, and listened to his 1981 non-smash hit, "The Property of Jesus". The gears began turning. I thought about my upcoming painting exhibition on hydrofracking, an adulthood of going my own way (always against the AARP grain), and strangely enough, my lifelong friend Pat and an expression he'd often share with me. (I'll get to that in a moment.)

Some righteous lyrics from the song "Property of Jesus":

Stop your conversation when he passes on the street
Hope he falls upon himself, oh, won't that be sweet
Because he can't be exploited by superstition anymore
Because he can't be bribed or bought by the things that you adore

When the whip that's keeping you in line doesn't make him jump
Say he's hard-of-hearin', say that he's a chump
Say he's out of step with reality as you try to test his nerve
Because he doesn't pay tribute to the king that you serve

Say that he's a loser 'cause he got no common sense
Because he don't increase his worth at someone else's expense
Because he's not afraid of trying, say he's got no style
'Cause he doesn't tell you jokes or fairy tales/
say things to make you smile

Boy, I know that feeling Dylan had and evoked with this song, and it's not just for the Born Again Christians, of which I am not one at present. It is radical, for humans anyway, in the sense that it is deeply rooted in our DNA and impossible to kill. It is the essence of individuality expressed as righteousness unto the clan. Society needs more individuality, not less. But not the kind that promotes itself, rather one that nurtures love of life, and right environment for all to share. Very difficult to love life from a cesspool. I believe that every healthy mind feels this way, that is, morally, upon waking up in the morning. At least one begins each day moral before the virtual onslaught of media mores, which sadly have become the norm in gaging how society behaves in public. That is, wholly dispassionate, quiet, careful, without opinion expressed outside of the everyday fact that "I am human", just as any streamlined institution says what it is depending on the product to be sold or the idea being disseminated; "I am fruit cocktail", or "Liberals are communists", or "I am Bob Dylan the wise old man who could afford a private nose-picker if desired". "The Property of Jesus" lyrics express what it truly means to be human among humans… Passionate for the betterment of all. And I don't see any age requirement. As a young born again Christian holding tightly to an easy millionaire's morality, Bob Dylan wasn't feeling ostracized because he rode around in private planes, but he sure as hell should feel that way now.

Okay, back to my friend Pat, and what he said to the opposite sex a few times when we were fourteen. He would walk up to a girl he knew, she might be opening her locker or sitting on the bleachers at a football game, and he would whisper by her ear, "Tickle your ass with a feather?"

The girl would exclaim, "What did you say?"

To which Pat immediately followed with, "Particularly nice weather?"

This memory pops into my head from time to time. I can't help it, the brain is a mysterious recollector. Anyway, I come home from the periodontist, all jacked up with angst and gum pain, and I start painting while day dreaming of what I really want to do to the gas men, which is, *tar and feather them*. Unfortunately, it's already late in the day. I have been AARP'd and orally violated to the point of my drool bib getting Pollocked all bloody, so my age begins to show by nightfall, and although I want the corporitos publically humiliated and dragged through the streets, I remember my media training in dispassion, and write instead,

Particularly Nice Weather, Tar and Tickle Texas Feather.

It's the safer way to keep eyes affixed to the painting. Even though it will hang at a gallery called "ArtRage", I am reminded by Bob Dylan and the AARP that it is foolhardy to make passionate expression at late middle age. Even if I have nothing to lose! Opinions are always suspected. Negative ones can place you in the order of fanatics. Once Bob Dylan expressed his belief in Jesus, he immediately became a fanatic to the cultured, dispassionate public. If I tell (or yell) my fracking woes too loudly, I will be deemed environmental fanatic. No one ever calls the gas lobbyist fanatical, maybe because he dons a suit and manicure, but what is he if not Mr. Fanatic himself, spending a life's profession pushing for just one platform? Even I, as painter, will go on to the next subject after ArtRage. We, as dispassionate Americans, allow this trespass on our families, without a fight. It is polite. Shhh. Quiet. It is best to pretend wisdom like Bob Dylan getting old.

After leaving the periodontist and coming home to paint, which is my passion, I realize now, more than yesterday, that AARP Magazine will never show on its cover the face of a sick child affected by water and air pollution produced by hydrofracking. They will continue to feature dispassionate people like Bob Dylan in his cool new hat. He won't mention hydrofracking either—his business people frown on political opinions generated by old millionaires. It upsets the purchasing climate. AARP would sell less Toyotas and prescription medications, and Bob Dylan would pass away wondering why nobody cared that he dreamed he was the septuagenarian idol of the bobby soxers.

I need to work on my passion. Not only is it the voice of wisdom, but it's all I have internally after a life lived loving Bob Dylan songs. When fifty, I'd rather be the property of a defunct Jesus, than belonging to the old age club that credentials anyone, even a pimp or pedophile, simply because they have hit a time marker. I hear tortoises and elephants can get into the AARP too, provided that they reach a ripe old age in captivity.

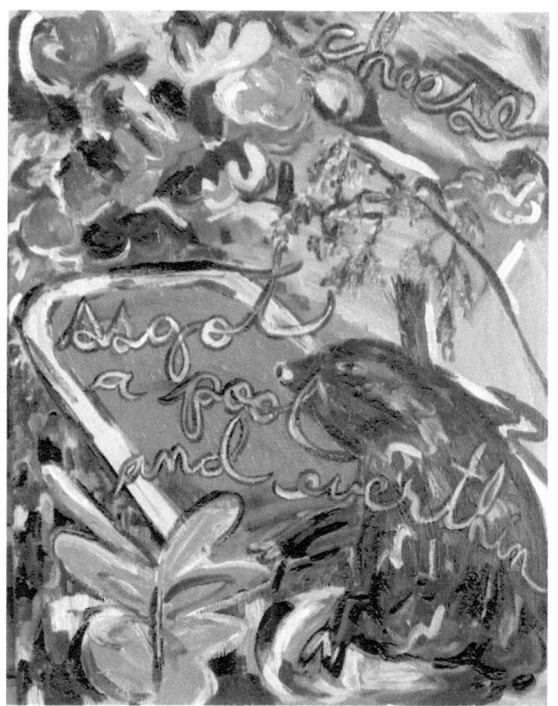

Cheese Ssgot a Pool and Everthin 2013.
Acrylic on canvas, 18 x 24"

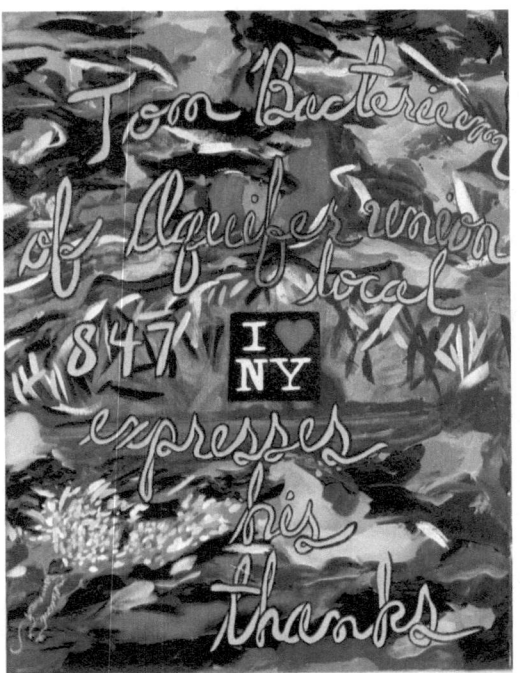

2014. Acrylic on canvas, 16 x 20"

Tom Bacterium of Aquifer Union Local 847 Expresses His Thanks

New York can now join Vermont in triumph. A boon to eco-tourism. Money can be made without injecting benzene into subterranean vaults of earth. The Finger Lakes region has breathed a sigh of Christmas relief. The Route 20 corridor will be more July beautiful than it has ever been. And the poor folks along the Southern Tier can remain poor like they have for the last 2,500 years. Nobody need sicken their kids with vanadium lemonade. The false promises of economy have finally lost a round. Dingding! Back to its sweaty corner where executives will lick their sour-puss wounds and find many new ways to hit below the belt. Pay off the referee. Wear down the opponent with poetic Ali propaganda. "More jobs mama! More wealth. New tractors and cars and stealth." "We can buy more Chinese crap, ironically, without knowing that the same folks wooing us now, mutilated our cash cow".

This holiday season, every non-edible present I purchased for loved ones was manufactured in another country. Those other countries own our national economy, and the expediting American CEO will have his butler wrap a custom made American yacht to place under the Christmas tree. The jobs were taken from us by legislation a generation ago. With this week's victory, all the ignorant, pretend job lovers of earth have learned that not everything is for sale for everyone. And by golly Mr. and Ms. Environmentalist, don't let your heads inflate. As soon as solar kicks in, China will become its sole producer. You will work at Lowe's and Walmart to sell photovoltaic everything. Both your toaster and Guatemalan coffee grinder can miraculously harvest energy from the sun. They will break a day after warranty, and you'll call India for service to be put on hold, which could make you late for your cashier's position at Lowe's, that is, if you weren't raised with such a strong work ethic foundation, the one every businessman would smash to bits out from under your feet if given the opportunity to add a penny to the bottom line.

It was easy money, wasn't it? "Drill, baby drill. Take rights to my land. I only live once. I am earth. I made God. Could have had a six pack in the fridge guaranteed until death did its part. Hot damn, it was easy money! Just a bad sniff once in a while... Maybe a kid or two snifflin' more than usual... But a new used truck! Damn tree huggers. They took my jawb!"

No. They took your easy money. They broke off a chip of your addiction to the trite and inane. They taught you a lesson for your own good, revitalized the future for your land where you had not one idea for it besides greed manifestation.

Dick Cheney and Satan 16   *Health and Happiness 1*

Game ain't over yet.

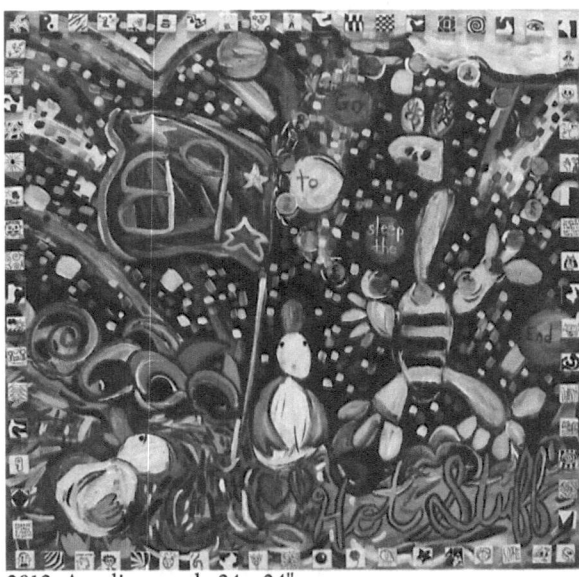

2012. Acrylic on oak, 24 x 24"

Go To Sleep The End

Who here remembers the Deepwater Horizon oil spill of 2010? Defective well cement, big methane explosion, eleven humans, and 111 billion other forms of life dead, Tony Haywood, the British Petroleum CEO at the time, wanting his life back…

I remember my "faith in good government coffin" getting wood-glued and screwed shut, buried deep, and covered. Each of the 87 days as oil gushed out of the sea floor, I became increasingly hostile toward a federal government that certainly knew how to dress itself in the morning, but held no real power, no matter what the finery. Smoke and mirrors controlled by the true, leading magicians. Power didn't come from a block of influential senators. Nor was it practiced by any President at the bully pulpit. Poor Barack Obama didn't have a clue what to do. To be fair, no President would have, because the real power need not listen to reason. The real power elects and rejects our leaders. The leaders know it. They try their best to save face. It works for the masses. It even works for me, who is most cynical of representative government. I know that today true protest can only come from an intelligent suffering body of people. And it cannot be pretty.

How is it that no representative of BP, Halliburton, or Transocean spent one night in a Mississippi jail cell, when just 50 years ago, simply being black and wanting to vote would land you there if you were lucky, or dead in a ditch if you weren't so? The entire gulf coast economy devastated by the greed of a few men, and those men got off scot-free, why? Because those men (mostly men remember), run your shadow government. We have let it happen, and only we can stop it.

A side anecdote: Back in 2006 I invited another stay-at-home dad over to my country house so the children could play. I was still wound up about the illegal invasion of Iraq and asked him what he thought about it. He replied with a statement that has sat in my stomach like a brick for the last nine years. It was this:

"Oh, I trust the folks in power know what's best for the country".

I remember that day well. I remember my "faith in humanity coffin" getting wood-glued and screwed shut, buried deep, and covered.

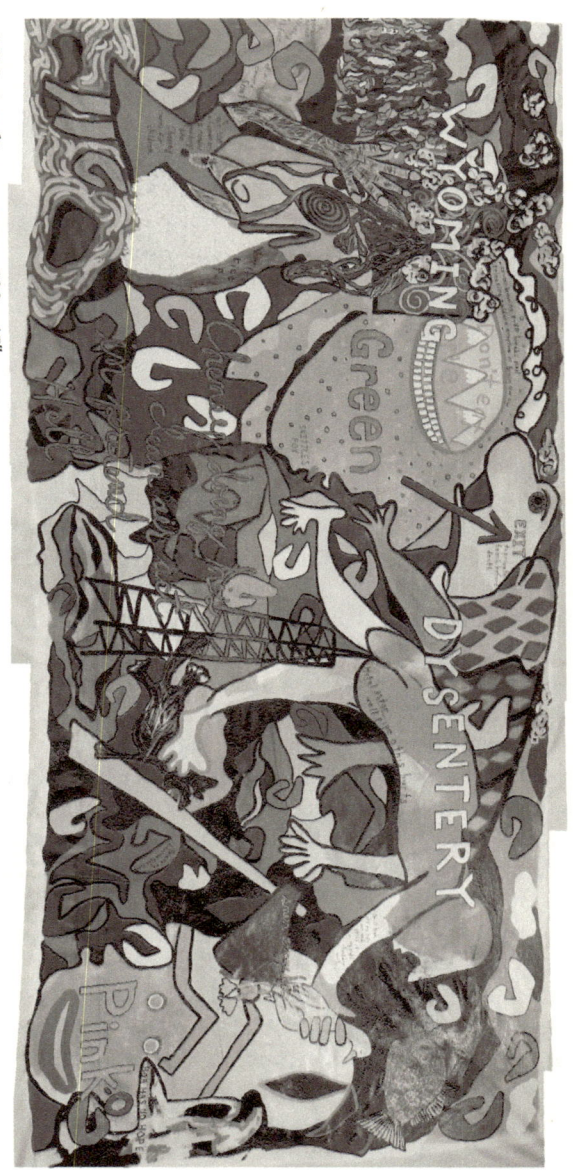

2015. Acrylic on canvas, 108 x 45"

Cheney Doing His Clean Air Act In Pretend Hell

"It's easy enough to tell what is wrong
but that's not what I want to hear all night long"
—Lou Reed from "New Sensations"

Okay. So Dick Cheney is going to hell. Granted, it's a pretend
hell, because real hell does not exist. One would think that if it did,
a frack well or two would hit a devil head on the way down and
cause a hot fracas.

Cheney knows there is no hell. There is the present moment. And
in the present moment he has power and is rich, and in tomorrow's
present moment he will be even richer. Maybe rich wouldn't be
so bad if, by association, Dick Cheney had refrained from killing
many people in undeclared and shadow warfare, or if his oil rig
didn't explode and dissolve eleven bodies in the ether, or if his nefarious manipulations of the Clean Air Act did not ensure a future
sickness to many school children.

So I made this painting to show all and sundry the truth about
justice in the secular world.

There is none. Ever. Period.

Yet I swear that people need to be reminded over and over this
truism. Dick Cheney is not the problem. The people are. They are
too nice, too forgiving, too live and let living. "Yeah, Cheney is
bad, but don't we all share those lower human qualities? Would
not many of us act just like Dick if encountering the same situa-
tions along life's road?"

Sure, if magically you became power and wealth in the present
moment. But you never will. You think you might get some spoils,
that your private, insignificant greed scam will pay off some day—
maybe with a white Lincoln Continental for retirement. Perhaps
a well lit Florida room in an affordable 55 and older community.
You sold mandated insurance at a ridiculous mark-up, but you
didn't kill anyone, so of course you have every right to cheat your
neighbor. Shhhh. Live and let live. You stay silent of Dick Cheney's
transgressions hoping that oligarchy has set aside a chance for

you too. Of course! Live and let live, even if one of the livers kills people indiscriminately. "Let God sort us out!"

This would be nice, but it isn't this way at all. You and I have no mortal chance to mirror Dick Cheney. There just isn't enough time in a life to develop his kind of misanthropy. To catch up, any adult would need a 72 hour day of taking advantage of others, while hating, and then killing some of them.

Well, could it be that Cheney lives the life of a tortured soul?

No. People with private planes do not have tortured souls. Maybe Jesus and Vincent van Gogh suffered an ever-present despair, but they often went hungry, and planes weren't invented in their time.

Hell is dead. But pretend hell is not. Living hell can only exist for those who are physically suffering, or have chemical imbalances that require chemicals prescribed for better balance.

So I made up this pretend hell for Cheney to perform his clean air act. Here the world is inundated by his own sneer. Hundreds of them, passing by constantly. I have Dick dress up in women's clothing, paint his nails fluorescent rose, break a nail, and have a caldera erupt in his brain. I have made him appear as a Titan from my daughter's manga series. He crushes a stuffed toy cat while squeezing a duck to death. There's even a Bob with no hope painted in to tell a joke about pretend hell.

And it is a joke, because at any time, Cheney can exit out of the canvas, and holiday on his private beach. Every year we pay our federal tax, we kiss the ring finger of one of the worst human beings ever de-wombed from a mother. The joke is us. The joke is justice. A man has manipulated the law called the "Clean Air Act", and we act like there is nothing to be done about it. We are not the people who seek a more perfect union. We are fools and cowards. We wait for bad men to do good things.

So, what is our energy future to be, even if we continue to allow the trespass of these dirty rotten scoundrels like Dick "the killer" Cheney?

If not fracking, then what? How do we achieve energy independence? And by independent, I mean local, or individual at best like your 4x great grandparents. They had wood, and then coal, and that was sufficient until the industrialists felt the greed need to mass produce shoes and then Happy Meal toys. Can the 21st century man live like mid-19th century man? I guess it doesn't matter, and there lies the problem… Today the people of western nations do not understand the seasons of survival. Their descendants will. It's going to get hot for all, including the top level consumers of tomorrow.

I don't know the answers about clean energy nor all the right questions to ask about the dirty stuff. I do know that the food and plastic waste at my new job cooking for the unappreciative elderly is a carbon footprint dense enough to press a hole six feet deep with each step toward extinction. And I thought I was a humble man! Should I mention the small crime I committed by taking the job in order to support my out-of-control acrylic painting habit? Humble, ha! I am a rotten neighbor stopped at the light, alone in my automobile, thinking about the next thing I shall acquire for me, whether it's concrete dioxine purple, or abstract holiday happiness, all illusions are locked onto the same vanity wheel, turning round and around.

A start is to stop and transport our minds five centuries into the past. Muse on the impossibility of global warming before China employed armies to build plastic toys for our dumbed-down sugar kids. Remember natural localism, the butcher and the baker, the thatch hut maker, harvest and holiday, and one hundred meaningful seasons in a year. The past will have to become the future if we want to sustain our humanity numbers and also grow grain to grind. The science devotees imagine they are alone in a warm room dreaming big while a magical god supplies them with all that neat stuff—lithium, titanium, steel, petroleum, millions of square meters of electro-goody-goodies—to one day colonize a comet and eat each other.

We can have the past right now with concentrated effort to supply good medicine (already invented) to all. To end nationalism and globalism overnight. To reinstate a very neighborly capitalism with the caveat "each family an acre to till and a central pasture outside the bastide".

The first man to weasel two acres gets burned at the stake.

Still, Neil Young wants you and I to boycott Starbucks for its collusion with Monsanto while he rushes off in a jet airplane to his concert in Reykjavík. If Neil Young can't be wise by now, I believe our only environmental salvation is a quick and easy nuclear winter to start up where Hieronymus Bosch left off, but replete with storehouses full of seeds, knowledge, antibiotics and well-trained Cuban doctors who get paid just a few hundred more pesos a week than a garbage collector.

Calisthenics for Tomorrow

Now that progeny is quaint
and financial schemes the wise
Threshing is the future exercise

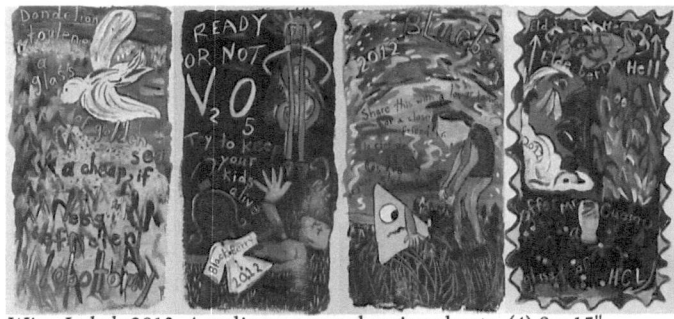

Wine Labels 2013. Acrylic on press cleaning sheets, (4) 8 x 15"

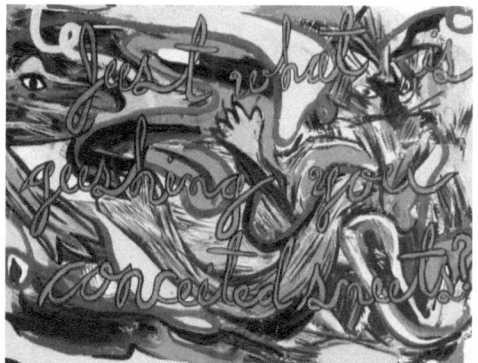

Just What is Gushing You Conceited Snuts? 2014.
Acrylic on canvas, 20 x 16"

The Last Painting

The last rage painting directed at politicos of my state is not
necessary, for the time being. This is a people win. No fracking in
New York! It is official. I knew all along my paintings would com-
pel the most obstinate snut (new word) in power to see the light.
Tonight I shall drink two gallons of water. And a tall bottle of my
homemade brew. And a glass of blackberry wine. I will soak up my
luscious New York water like an eager sponge. Hurray! The fascists
are leaving our territory. The northeast is the new west. No goose
step during this political cycle.

But it's just a matter of time before we lose our state to the wild
west greed of the very few.